A Victorian Convert Quintet

DEDICATION

This work is dedicated to the Community of Downside Abbey without whose hospitality and help it could never have been written.

A Victorian Convert Quintet

Studies in the Faith of Five Leading Victorian Converts to Catholicism from the Oxford Movement.

MICHAEL CLIFTON

The Saint Austin Press
London, 1998.

THE SAINT AUSTIN PRESS
296, Brockley Road,
London,
SE4 2RA.

ISBN 1 901157 03 2

A catalogue record for this book is available from the British Library

Printed in Great Britain by BPC Wheatons, Exeter.

ACKNOWLEDGMENTS.

I would like to thank Fr. Ian Dickie, Archivist of the Archdiocese of Westminster, Fr. Henry Parker CSSR the Archivist of the English Province of the Redemptorists, The Librarians at Mitcham Public Library, Surrey, Balliol and Magdalen Colleges, Oxford and of course Dom Philip Jebb, and Dom Daniel Rees O.S.B. of Downside, for the use of their libraries and archives.

Contents

Preface

In this book I am attempting to trace the journeys in faith of five very distinguished converts of the Oxford Movement who are however largely forgotten today.

The reader may well ask "Why these five ?" The answer is that after their conversion to Catholicism their "Faith Stories" went in very different directions. At one end there is the extreme ultramontanist Robert Coffin, English Provincial of the Redemptorists for many years,and confidant of Cardinal Manning, while at the other end of the scale is St.George Mivart who ended his life excommunicated for heresy. The remaining three line up in between.

However that would not explain why I have selected these five individuals in particular. My thoughts on the subject started with Robert Coffin who became the third Bishop of Southwark and I have already written biographies of Thomas Grant and Peter Amigo, two other Bishops of my diocese. Simpson interested me because he was at one time Rector of Mitcham, next door to the Parish I work in. Richard Sibthorp interested me as one who kept on switching between Anglicanism and Catholicism, Mivart had interested me since my student days as the author of a pamphlet entitled *Happiness in Hell* while Oakeley was of interest as the translator of the carol *O come all ye faithful.*

I discovered too that there are many interesting links between them. They all knew each other quite well except for Mivart and Sibthorp. More importantly they were all in correspondence with John Henry Newman at one time or another. The influence of French Emigré clergy on their lives is of interest. Sometimes too, the same places keep cropping up in their lives, particuarly Clapham, where both Simpson and Coffin lived most of their lives. One of the most extraordinary links is that all of them (except Mivart) had dealings of one type or another with Charles Sumner, Bishop of Winchester.

It is not the purpose of this work to give full biographies of any of these subjects. Biographies already exist for Simpson, Mivart and Sibthorp. A Biography in Manuscript is to be found in the provincial archives of the Redemptorists for Coffin. No full study of the life of Frederick Oakeley exists though he wrote several autobiographical articles. My object is to explore the development of their faith. I have tried to use as much unpublished material as possible plus articles which are not widely available for reading today.

Finally I hope their stories will be of benefit to the reader today who will be able to trace many of the curent problems in the Church back to the last century.

MC
April, 1998

PART ONE
Robert Aston Coffin
Confidant of Cardinal Manning

Introduction

Most of biographical detail for Robert Coffin is taken from the Manuscript Life by Fr. Lubienski CSSR. written in French but partly translated into English which is kept in the Provincial archives of the English Redemptorists at Clapham. A further source at Clapham is a shorter Memoir almost certainly written by Fr. Bridgett CSSR also found only as a Manuscript The text will indicate in particular where I quote from Bridgett rather than Lubienski.

CHAPTER ONE. *Early Life.*

Robert Aston Coffin was born at Brighton, Sussex on the 19th July 1819. His father was Robert Coffin and his mother Elizabeth Nash.

The Lubienski document claims that Robert senior was the son of Isaac Coffin, 1st (and last) Baronet. However Isaac, a somewhat eccentric naval captain, had no children and his title died with him. In fact Robert senior would appear to be the son of one Thomas Aston Coffin, a commissary General to H.M. Troops serving in Great Britain, who died in 1810 and left the residue of his large estate to his natural son Robert who was then still at Oxford.

As a result of his inheritance, Robert, the father of the future Bishop, never had to do any work at all and lived entirely off invested income and rents. Elizabeth his wife was born in Oporto, daughter of a wine merchant. As a young girl she had been tutored by a French Emigré priest, but never became a Catholic. Apparently the French Emigré priest was given the work on the condition he made no attempt to interfere with her religion. She was very devout and the future Bishop always spoke of her with great respect. She died in 1865 and Robert was with her. He related that he made no attempt to induce a deathbed conversion but recited acts of faith hope and charity with her. He also told Lubienski that in 1881 he was giving a retreat at a convent where a certain sister was known to have received extraordinary favours from God. She made her confession to Coffin and at the end just added. "Your mother is saved". She had no knowledge whatever of his mother.

The family lived at Brighton on the Parade quite near the Catholic Church of St. John the Baptist. Robertwas baptised in the drawing room of the house in accordance with the custom of the time for rich Anglicans. He was named after St. Robert of Newminster but later preferred to commemorate the time he became a Catholic on the 3rd December, the feast of St. Francis Xavier to whom he had a great devotion.

The Coffin's had a total of four children, in order, Elizabeth, Robert, Edmond, and Henriette. Their father was a member of one of the most respected families in Brighton and Robert at the age of 6 was invited to a children's Ball given by the King at the famous Brighton Pavilion. At the same age he was placed with an Anglican Clergyman named Mr Edle who lived near Worthing and received into his house about six children "of the wealthy variety" to whom he gave lessons in Latin Greek and English. While studying with Mr Edle he was confirmed by Charles Sumner, Bishop of Winchester [1].

Robert was sent in 1834 to Harrow. It was here some years earlier that Manning had studied. However at this time the school was in decline. Discipline was lax and beatings still common. He was placed luckily in the Headmaster's house. The head was Charles Longley who later became Archbishop of Canterbury. He was known as being very devout but rather ineffective as a headmaster. Robert does not seem to have been happy at Harrow. Lubienski records that he cried at departing at the start of each term and wrote to his mother every single day. He was however developing his lifelong love of music. When asked at Harrow what he would like to be he replied "An actor at the opera or better a Bishop." At least his wish in that regard was fulfilled!

At this time his sole contact with Catholicism was by way of the Butler family of Blackheath in South London. Mr Butler had been a friend of the Nash family in Oporto and the two familes it seems often travelled together.

After two years at Harrow his father withdrew him because he found the expenses of his young family were too high. Dr. Longley advised that he take a private tutor to finish his education before going up to Oxford. Lubienski does not record who this tutor was but Fr. Bridgett in his memoir does state that it was yet another Anglican Clergyman. He entered Christ Church Oxford in 1837 and graduated BA with 3rd class honours in Classics in 1840. We do not know very much about his years at Oxford before 1840, but Bridgett recalls that he had an introduction to John Henry Newman right from the start. Later on Lubienski tells us that his friendship with Newman was like a love between father and son and that he was "The child of his Heart". It was Newman who told him about the advantages of celibacy and suggested to him that he take orders. Presumably that was after two occasions on which he nearly "fell into the trap" of marrying. It seems he was on holiday with the daughter of Mr Dalgairns (sister of the future Oratorian). Towards the end of their stay in Guernsey he was asked by his host what his intentions were, as it was understood that he would shortly be asking for the hand of his daughter. He replied "That cannot be. I wish to be a priest" and promptly returned to Oxford. Lubienski relates that by 1840 he had acquired rooms at the college and his quarters became the focus of a circle of friends often of the highest nobility. They were lovers of music for Coffin was gifted with a beautiful voice and played the piano like a master.

In his vacations he would travel from house to house

amongst his friends and enjoyed particularly concerts and walking. Under Newman he learnt to always seek after perfection.

Neither Lubienski nor Bridgett can tell us what exactly Coffin did between 1840 and 1843 when he took Anglican Orders from Dr. Bagot. He did not try for a fellowship but certainly remained in Oxford.

After receiving orders he lost no time in applying directly for the benefice of St. Mary Magdalen's Church in Oxford. The benefice was in the hands of his college it seems. So at the tender age of 24 he had first taste of being a religious superior. This parish church is of interest, part of it having been built by St Hugh of Lincoln in the twelfth century. The Church was frequented by professors and students of the University and many rich personalities from the town. Now, under the guidance of John Henry Newman, Coffin had moved right away from the evangelical stance of his earlier years. Indeed he had strong differences with his first curate Mr Hathaway which led to that gentleman removing elsewhere. Later Mr Hathaway became a Catholic and an eminent Jesuit. His next curate Mr Collins, was from the start more on the same wavelength and followed Robert into the Catholic Church also becoming a Jesuit in time. It was said of Coffin at this time that he was preaching Catholic Doctrine and holding nothing back. He never took up residence with Newman at Littlemore but would often visit him there. Before he finally decided to become a Catholic he was already creating a stir by preaching Catholic Doctrines. In 1844 he visited his father, then living near Bognor and the local vicar, none other than his former tutor, Mr Edle, invited him to preach. His sermon was on the real presence of Our Lord in the Blessed Sacrament. This led one parishioner to walk out and write to the Press:

> "I left the Church when I heard false doctrines preached by Mr Robert Coffin who tried to impress on communicants that when they receive the sacrament of the Lord's Supper that they actually eat Christ's

Body and drink his Blood. This I considered... to lead us step by step to Popery...and although his doctrine was so repugnant to the feelings of many, still Mr Edle persisted in forcing this young man upon us the following Sunday and sat and heard him abuse those who had dared or presumed to leave the Church the previous Sabbath rather than remain and hear Popish teaching."

It is however recorded that when a year later Mr Edle heard of Coffin's defection to Rome, he wept bitterly and lamented the fall of the young soldier.

CHAPTER TWO. Conversion and the Oratory.

During the course of 1845 many of Coffin's friends left Anglicanism for the Catholic Faith. However even when Dr. Newman was received by Fr Dominic, he did not consider joining him. He continued his work at St.Mary Magdalen's. A short time later though, Fr. Lubienski relates that a particular incident in the Parish led him to change his mind.

A lady in the Parish lay dying and in the absence of the curate who was her regular confessor she called for Mr Coffin. When Mr Coffin started the words of absolution in the Anglican form "May God absolve you" she interrupted him saying "You don't know whether you are a priest or not" She declared her desire to see a Catholic Priest instead and Mr Coffin obliged by seeking out the Catholic Missioner of Oxford, Fr.Newsham, to call on her. She was duly received into the Catholic Church and died shortly after. The Press got to hear the story and the local churchwardens called on their rector to explain his actions. He duly showed them the door! But the words of the people, "The Vicar was with the sick person at 11.00am and the Priest at midday" caused Coffin to think that after all he wasnot a true priest. Shortly after this his mother came to visit him at Oxford. She had heard that he might already have "defected" to Rome. She stayed about a month trying to persuade him to stay at his post. During this time his mind was finally made up and he decided to take one month' leave, asking his friend Frederick Oakeley to stand in. At this time Oakeley had left his position as Rector at Margaret Street.

A few days later he told his parents that he had made up his mind to join the Catholic Church. His father persuaded him first to visit Dr.Pusey the well known Anglican theologian. He told him that it was impossible for him to remain in the Anglican communion. Pusey could only say that it was all "very sad". Coffin's father then suggested he might just resign his benefice and continue to live as an anglican at Oxford. Perhaps Dr. Manning could help him. So Coffin duly went to see the illustrious Archdeacon of Chichester. Instead of meeting him directly he met up with Miss Lockheart and rather afraid of meeting his fellow ex-Harrovian, he asked the good lady to put to Dr Manning the question "May one who believes all the dogmas of the Catholic Church remain a Protestant and not become a Catholic ?" Miss Lockheart returned with the simple answer "He who believes all the dogmas of the Catholic Church ought to become a Catholic"

Yet it was another three weeks before Coffin made his final move.

One day while still in bed he received a letter from Dr. Newman who had enclosed a medal of the Immaculate Conception and begged him to wear it. "Scarcely had he put on the medal" relates Fr. Lubienski, "than his doubts disappeared and he saw clearly what God wished him to do." Coffin spent the entire day writing letters to his superiors and others that he was about to join the Catholic Church. He then announced the same news to his people.

Shortly after this, Dr Newman and Mr St.John returned to Oxford after their reception into the Church. It was now late November 1845. Coffin went to visit his old friend and Newman asked him why he had not become a Catholic. He told Lubienski later "I can see him now putting down his spectacles and while continuing to converse with me taking up Bradshaw (the Railway timetable) and examining it. Then he said there was a train to Bath in the afternoon. Would I like to come to Prior Park with him and there be received into the Church ? 'Very well,' replied Coffin and the business was arranged."

On arrival at Prior Park, the party was greeted by Coffin's old curate Mr Collins, now a fervent neophyte. Monsignor Brindle, the Vicar Apostolic of the region interviewed the new candidate.

Brindle.. "What do you desire ?"

Coffin .. "I desire to be received into the Catholic Church"

Brindle.. "Have you any doubts or difficulties about our dogmas?"

Coffin.. "None whatever"

Brindle.. "Very well. This morning at 11.00 we shall have your reception into the Church."

It was the 3rd December. Assisting the Bishop was Fr. William Vaughan, later first Bishop of Plymouth. Also present was a young cleric, Clifford, who later became Bishop of Clifton diocese. He made his first Holy Communion on the Feast of the Immaculate Conception.

Right from the time he left Oxford he had decided on becoming a Priest but had no inclination to become a secular Priest. So on advice he waited a while and in February 1846 he took up a post as tutor for one year to the children of Ambrose Phillips de Lisle, himself a convert who was much devoted to the cause of Christian unity. During the Summer he went on holiday with the family and they passed through Belgium. Here Mr Coffin made his first direct contact with the Redemptorist order which he later joined. At this time however he had no thoughts of joining the order which indeed had no English members then.

His contract to tutor the children of Ambrose Philipps de Lisle was only for one year and he never intended to continue in this task. So in Febrary 1847 he set out for Rome in company with Mr McMullen who had been with him at St Mary Magdalen's for a few weeks as a temporary curate. McMullen also had become a Catholic and would later become a secular priest and Canon of the Westminster Diocese. For many years he was Rector at Cadogan Place, Chelsea. It is interesting to note here that he was one of the few priests (as opposed to laymen) who supported the Liberal Catholic Movement later on.

Coffin intended to ask Newman about his vocation in the future and on arrival found that Newman had come to the decision to join the congregation of the Oratory and to introduce that congregation into England. Newman felt that in starting up the Oratorians, he could keep together at least some of his closest followers from the Oxford days in community. The Oratorian life appealed, as it allows more freedom for the individual than does any religious order and the Oratorians are not bound to a vow of poverty but retain all their existing wealth. Their apostolate is usually parochially based with both spiritual direction and ordinary parish duties combined. The Oratorian way of life and spirituality is based on the life and writings of their founder, St. Philip Neri.

Coffin decided to join Newman after making a retreat with the Jesuit Fr. Grassi. He joined Newman who was accompanied by St.John, Dalgairns, Penny and Bowles in temporary rooms at Santa Croce where they lived a semi-monastic life. During the Summer they prepared for the priesthood. On October 12th Coffin and Penny passed their examination for Holy Orders and received the diaconate together on October 24th. One week later Coffin received the Priesthood. His ordination took place during the noviciate of three months which the Roman Oratory prescribed for the converts.

Coffin left Rome to return to England. On the way home he stayed in Bruges with his family and there made the acquaintance of Fr Paul Reyners, the Redemptorist who would later be his novice master. Coffin had already studied many of the works of the Redemptorist founder St. Alphonsus Liguori and it can be said that at this stage there arose the first beginnings of doubt over his future vocation as an Oratorians.

When the converts were assembled in England the English Oratory was formally established by a Brief of Pope Pius IX on February 2nd, 1848, the Feast of the Purification. (now known as the Presentation of Our Lord). Fr Newman was appointed Superior and Fr Coffin as Fr Minister and one of the four deputies or consultors to the Superior.

To start with the entire group lived at Old Oscott College, now known as Maryvale. There were 29 in all including lay brothers. Shortly after this, Fr. Faber joined the Oratory with his recently established community of "Wilfridians". At this point Newman transferred the entire community to St. Wilfred's at Cotton in Staffordshire where there was a particularly beautiful church.

In the Spring of 1848 Bishop Wiseman asked Newman to provide preachers for the Lenten sermons in the principal London Churches, St George's Southwark, Cadogan St, and Spanish Place. Newman shared this work with Coffin, Dalgairns, and Hutchinson but it was an almost total failure with empty churches being the order of the day!

Coffin was present at the opening of St George's Cathedral in London. The opening ceremony was the most spectacular religious event to take place in the capital since the passing of Catholic Emancipation and was widely reported. However Coffin wrote to a friend on June 3rd: "We have been much amused with the *Times* account of the opening of St George's; What seems to have struck them most was the extraordinary ugliness of the 200 or so clergy present." [2]

During 1848 Newman was preparing plans for the extension of the Oratorian work to Birmingham and London. On February 2nd 1849 the Oratory was set up in Birmingham (at Alcester Street). Fr. Coffin then became superior at St. Wilfred's. In the next few weeks there was much discussion as to who would form the new London Community. To start with it was thought that Coffin would move there as Superior but in May 1849 Fr.Faber went to London as the new superior taking with him most of the remaining Fathers and novices.[3].

Fr. Coffin was now in a difficult position. When St Wilfred's started up as an Oratory, there was work there amongst the people but now Fr Newman wanted him to start up a school and sent boys to St Wilfred's nominating Coffin as headmaster. Coffin told Newman that to start a school was going straight against the spirit of the Institute of St Philip. [4]. The school started up but now Fr. Coffin was most unhappy. He decided to make a retreat with the Rememptorist Fr. Lans at nearby Hanley. The attractions of the Remptorist life were becoming strong but he wished to ascertain the will of God before joining.

In the Summer of 1849 he made a general confession to Fr.Lans and asked to be admitted to the Order. Fr Lans correctly gave him no encouragement and advised him to continue at St.Wilfred's.

Shortly after this Bishop Ullathorne came to confirm the boys and Coffin confided in him his desire to join the Redemptorists. After hearing the reasons adduced for leaving the Oratorians, Ullathorne agreed that he should become a Redemptorist.

Now the rumours of the possible defection of Fr Coffin reached Newman and Faber. Two fathers from London came up to see him and tried to persuade him to change his mind but in vain. The first that Newman knew about Coffin's decision was on October 3rd when Fr Nicholas visited Newman with a letter from Coffin. Coffin had been ordered up to London because the Fathers of the London House would be meeting that day. Coffin had replied that he did not wish to go to London and that he was intending to join the Redemptorists. He considered that there was no tradition of Spiritual life in the Oratory. Newman replied that he would like Coffin to go to the Florentine Oratory to study the spirituality and theology of the Congregation for a period of years and then come back and start a new oratory possibly in Clifton. [5].

On October 9th the documents were signed that officially separated the London House from Birmingham. St

Wilfred's community was to be transferred to London, and the boys education stopped. St Wilfred's would simply continue as a mission served by an Oratorian.

On the 2lst November Coffin wrote to Newman that he had definitely resolved "to leave the world and enter religion as a Redemptorist". He hoped "that I may leave the world with the knowledge of your good will towards me."

On the 22nd Newman wrote a kind letter back: "I can never be distressed at anyone being called to what he considers a more religious life than he is leading at Priest.....we all send our love."

Yet only two days later he writes again to Coffin:

"...now I distinctly state if you have not already gathered it from my last letter to you that in reality I have no sympathy with what you are doing." On the very same day he wrote a long letter to Faber listing all the complaints about the Oratory that Coffin is said to have made. Coffin is said to have alleged that St Philip Neri was making the oratory into an easy club, that the Oratorian fathers at London had little experience and that their system of internal house retreats was quite wrong. Newman ends up by saying "I think he is possessed of a bad spirit...whether it will improve matters to bring him to London I cannot tell..for he is cantankerous...broods over imaginary insults,slights and difficulties, feels he will be a stranger in London." [6]

On the 23rd November Faber summoned Coffin to come to London at once. Faber told him that pride was at the bottom of his decision. He tried for two hours to persuade him to change his mind but at the end Coffin said "You can overwhelm me with words but have not convinced me. Let me go to Fr. Lans and I will follow his advice." Father Faber agreed but suggested he should pay a visit to Fr Dalgairns for they were intimate friends. He had to be up early on the Sunday morning to catch the solitary train. The weather was foul and he had a splitting headache. Furthermore he was racked with doubts and temptations.

At Paddington he heard the consoling news "You will have to wait six hours Sir, at Swindon." He suffered a most appalling inner desolation and in one dreadful moment considered it would better to be rid of life altogether. He walked around in the rain for a considerable time without even realising it was raining. Once the train arrived he was more peaceful and when the next day came and he finally arrived at Hanley he spoke of his decision to Fr. Lans. Even then at this late stage Fr.Lans was unwilling to accept him at once but told him to stay with Fr. Faber for a further two years. He prepared a letter for Fr. Faber but before it could be posted a letter arrived from Fr. Faber informing Coffin he was released and could preach his final sermon the following Sunday at St. Wilfred's. Fr. Lans told him to go first to see Fr Newman at Birmingham and bid him farewell. This was for both a very painful meeting. The bonds of friendship had been severed. Father Bridgett relates that Newman's last words to Coffin were "I can forgive you but I can never forget". As far as I can discover they never met or corresponded after this meeting except that Coffin sent Newman congratulations on the publication of the Apologia pro Vita Sua, and Newman sent Coffin a telegram of condolence as he lay dying at Teignmouth many years later.

Newman's judgement on Coffin's behaviour at this time may be considered as rather unfair. Newman relied on the word of his fellow Oratorian , Stanton, who visited Coffin at the start of these final events. Stanton told Faber (who then told Newman) that Coffin was under the direction of the Belgian Baron von Schroeter. This gentleman had been invited to stay at the Birmingham Oratory to paint a picture of the Oratorians. It was claimed that he had told Coffin that he considered the Oratorians too lax. As soon as Newman had heard Stanton's report, he wrote to the Baron telling him to pack his bags and go home at once. He accused him of being a real nuisance to the community and hinted at moral depravity as well.[7] In a footnote to the entry for November 28th Newman also relates that he considered that Coffin left the Oratorians because neither Birmingham nor London suited him. "Not London because he wanted to be with the Father (Newman), not Birmingham because he wanted NOT to be with Fr. Ambrose." Newman cannot have been aware of the soul-searching and pressures upon Fr. Coffin before he was able to come to the final decision to move. It should be remembered that Coffin had been under the influence of Newman since he was 18 years old. He had helped him with his *Lives of the British Saints* in writing the life of St.Wilfred. Perhaps Fr. Coffin should have confided in Newman earlier his thoughts about the Redemptorists.

CHAPTER 3. Into the Redemptorist Order.

After preaching his final sermon at St. Wilfred's, Coffin spent a few days with Fr. Lans at Hanley then crossed the channel to Belgium where he entered the Noviciate of the Redemptorists at St. Trond. His novice master was Fr. Paul Reyners. Rev. Edmund Vaughan, then a deacon entered with him on the same day, December 24th 1850. They received the habit together on 2nd February 1851. There were at the time in the Noviciate 25 novices of whom 11 were priests. There were seven Englishmen there, Frs. Coffin, Bradshaw, Plunkett, Bridgett, Stevens, Francis and Vaughan. Bridgett tells us that he went through the noviciate with great fervour and self sacrifice. Here was a man of distinguished talent who had been in a position of authority both as Anglican Vicar and as an Oratorian, descended to the level of the youngest simple novice.

He must have had much to suffer. The diet was meagre, the winter cold intense, some of his companions had rude manners, he had to learn to make a set of new friends. He was separated for ever from his past life.

On the 2nd February 1852 along with Fr. Vaughan as he now was, he made his profession. He spent a few more months in Belgium at Wittem and Liege before returning to England in July. He was initially appointed to the house at

Bishop Eton which had only been founded one year earlier. He was soon at work giving missions. He was sent over to the North of Ireland in September and gave his first mission at Enniskillen in September followed by Londonderry in October, Letterkenny in November and Omagh in January 1853. On his return to England he was posted to Clapham where he arrived on February 3rd 1853 and where he lived in effect for the rest of his life. It might be well at this point to consider what the Redemptorist vocation involved at this time.

St Alphonsus the founder of the order was born near Naples in 1696 and gifted with a remarkable intelligence was awarded a doctorate in both Civil and Canon Law at the age of 16. He was entitled to practice as a barrister but while still a youth and acting as senior counsel in a financial case involving a vast sum of money, it was shown that he had made a mistake and the case was lost. He left the courts and vowed never to return. He would put his talents solely at the service of Almighty God. He trained for the priesthood and sought particularly in his diocese to minister to the needs of those whom he considered most neglected, in this case, shepherds in the remoter parts of the region. After his health broke down he was resting when he came across a convent where supernatural happenings were frequent. One nun told Alphonsus that he was to be the founder of a new order and so the order of Redemptoristine nuns was started. Alphonsus now felt impelled to start an order for priests. However his chosen first few companions all deserted him and he had make a start all over again. The specific aim of his society was the formation of saints amongst its members and the exercise of the apostolate to abandoned souls. His institute spread throughout Italy but there were many set backs and when he died in 1787 there was a congregation hopelessly divided. This dire position was soon rectified by another saint who joined the order at the right time, St. Clement Hofbauer.[8]

The order became particularly strong in Belgium

thanks to the efforts of Fr. de Held, the first provincial of the Belgian province and a follower of St. Clement Hofbauer, From Belgium the foundations were made in the United States, Canada and Great Britain. The start in England was in 1843 at Falmouth but that mission had to be abandoned and the real beginnings of the great apostolate came with the foundation at Clapham in South London. Once Clapham was under way, the giving of missions became the main work of the English fathers. The rule of life for the Redemptorist is neither purely contemplative nor entirely active but combines both aspects. St Alphonsus tells us that the members of the order should "live neither for themselves nor for the people alone, but they should devote themselves first to their own sanctification by the practice of prayer and of all the virtues, and then to the sanctification of others."He described their lives as "Apostles abroad, Carthusians at home" Their motto as it were is that "Love is the chain of gold that binds souls to God and binds them so strongly that they seem unable to separate themselves from him." The foundation at Clapham is given as 1848. In the previous year a community of religious known as the "Filles de Marie" had obtained a property called St Ann's House in Clapham Old Town. At the same time Fr. de Held came up to London on some business and met with a Mr Philip at Spanish Place Church . Philip advised de Held to see Bishop Wiseman and the Bishop urged on de Held the need for a foundation in London. De Held had earlier held out against a move to London on the grounds that the primitive Redemptorists should work in poor country areas. Meanwhile Mr Philip made enquiries and informed De Held that a suitable property was available in Clapham at the corner of Acre Lane.

The property was bought for £1,000.00 down with £3,000.00 on mortgage.

After a short stay with the Filles de Marie until the house was ready for occupation, the first fathers moved in on the 3lst July. A small chapel was constructed inside the house which soon proved inadequate and then providence intervened again. The Rev. Edward Douglas who was at the time in the Noviciate at St.Trond heard of the problem and obtained permission to devote a portion of his family fortune to the building of a new Church. Mr William Wardell, a noted architect and disciple of Pugin, was commissioned and the fine Church of St. Mary's was put up. The house at Clapham was declared a Rectorate on the 18th February 1850 and the church was opened and consecrated on May 14th 1851.

The house occupied by the Fathers had an interesting history all of its own. Around the turn of the century there lived in Clapham a number of very distinguished persons. Chief amongst these was William Wilberforce who lived at Broomwood on the West Side of the Common.

Others resident in the locality included Zachary Macaulay, father of Lord Macauley, and Sir John Shore, later Lord Teignmouth and Governor General of India. Then there were the Thornton brothers. Stephen lived in the house occupied later by the first Redemptorists and his brother Samuel in a property backing on the same house at the rear. In 1800 Samuel entertained Pitt and others at a huge banquet. Then Lord Teignmouth took over Samuel's home and the first meetings of the Bible Society were held there. The objects of the society were the abolition of slavery, the diffusion of the Bible and the propagation of Christianity amongst the Heathen. As so many of its members lived there the society became well known as the "Clapham Sect". [9]

CHAPTER 4. *First Years at Clapham.*

When Fr Coffin arrived in Clapham the Rector was Fr. de Held and the Vice Rector Fr Reyners, his old novice master. De Held was often away and Reyners was not in good health. Reyners used Coffin to assist him right from his arrival. He had the utmost confidence in him from his time as novice. Coffin still found time to give missions and was at Scarborough in April and at the military camp at

Chobham in August where he gave a mission to the soldiers.

In January 1854 Father Reyners was made Rector of Clapham and he appointed Coffin as Minister which office he held until his own nomination as Rector. During the year he found time to take part in missions at Barntown, Co Wexford, St Finbar's Cork and Slindon in Sussex. During 1854 Holland, England, and Ireland were constituted a Vice Province and Domestic and Provincial Chapters were ordered to take place in preparation for the big general chapter in Rome. The Domestic chapter was held at Clapham on October 11th and Coffin was elected Vocal Deputy to accompany Fr Rector to the Provincial Chapter in Belgium. In 1855 Coffin took part a great mission in Dublin and his instruction given to 3000 young men in the course of the mission made such an impression that he was asked to give a separate retreat to that group alone following on from the mission. For a short while after, Coffin was attached to Bishop Eton in order that he could give missions in the North of England and during the Summer he gave two clergy retreats to the priests of the diocese of Hexham. He was recalled to Clapham in Septmber due to the serious illness of Fr Reyners. Fr Reyners was obliged to leave Clapham and Coffin was appointed Rector of Clapham.

Becoming Rector in no way lessened the demands on him for giving missions and retreats. During the year he took part in eight missions all over the country and gave retreats to the clergy of Hexham, Liverpool and Plymouth. He also started an apostolate of instructing Anglican Clergy prior to their reception into the Church. So successful was he in this work that he became known as the "Parson Slayer"!

In 1857 he took part in only two missions but gave several retreats and in the years that followed he concentrated almost exclusviely on retreats rather than missions. He gave his first retreat to students at Ushaw that year and introduced them to the method of meditation suggested by St.Alphonsus. The next few years saw much the same kind of programme. In 1859 he was given the additional role of Vice Provincial for the Vice Provincialate of Holland and England. The effects of his exertions were however beginning to tell. In 1862 his health broke down and he had to spend 5 months in Rome but even while recovering he found time to give retreats at the English and American Colleges. In 1864 his health broke down again and he was obliged to seek treatment at Aix la Chapelle.

At this point it may be well to examine the type of spirituality that Coffin was trying to impart in his missions and retreats.

The Redemptorists of course have had in the past a well known reputation for "hell-fire preaching." Certainly the fear of hell would play a large part in the preaching of that time but Coffin found that particularly in the towns, thousands of Catholics were lapsed ill instructed immigrants, and with the message of St.Alphonsus in mind he found it very necessary to inisist on a return to the practice of the faith. If the only way for the point to be pressed home was by fear of hell, then that would have to be preached.

I have not been able to trace the texts of any talks that Coffin gave either as missions or retreats but the archives of Southwark contain a poster advertising the programme for a retreat given by Fr Coffin to the Confraternity of the Holy Family. This was billed as a "Course of Spiritual Exercises for men".There was a note at the end:"Protestants also are admitted but no females will be allowed to attend". The course was held at 7.30pm each day and the subjects of the evening sermons were as follows:

Monday Evening. The Great Business of Life
Tuesday The Great Evil of Life.
Wednesday The General Judgement
Thursday The Eternity of Punishment
Friday The Passion of Jesus Christ.
Saturday No Sermon.
(Perhaps after hearing the earlier sermons the

congregation would be lining up for confessions!)

Fr Coffin did not merely limit himself to preaching in the spirit of St Alphonsus. During the 1850s he also translated most of his spiritual works into English and provided introductions.

One of these books is entitled *Preparation for Death* and by way of introduction Coffin explains to the reader the Alphonsan method of meditation. The method is now accepted as a standard method of making a meditation. Fr Coffin's explanation is quite concise and bears repetition here.

> "It consists of three parts, the Preparation, the Meditation and the Conclusion. In the preparation are contained three acts, viz. of faith, in the presence of God, of humility, and petition for light. By saying thus, 1) O my God I believe that Thou art present with me and I adore Thee from the abyss of my nothingness, 2) My Lord, I ought on account of my sins to be now dwelling in hell; I am sorry that I have offended thee, spare me for the sake of thy goodness. 3) Eternal Father for the sake of Jesus and Mary, give me light in this meditation that I may receive from it profit for my soul.
>
> Then say a Hail Mary that She may obtain this light, and Glory be to the Father, in honour of St. Joseph, your guardian angel and holy patrons. These acts should be made attentively but briefly and then at once proceed to the meditation.
>
> For meditation it is best for those who can read to use a book, pausing where the mind finds itself most affected...here we must observe that the spiritual profit derived from mental prayer does not consist so much in meditation as in making affections, petitions and resolutions; these are the three fruits of meditation. And so after reflecting on some eternal maxim, and after God has spoken to the heart, we ought ourselves to speak to God with the heart, by making affections or by acts of faith, of thanksgiving, of adoration, humility and most of all love and of contrition which is also an act of love. For love is the golden bond which unites the soul to God.

St Thomas teaches that every act of love obtains for us one degree of eternal glory; every single act of love merits eternal life. Now these are acts of love; to say, 'My God I prefer Thee above all things,... With my whole heart I love thee...Behold here I am, do with me and all belonging to me as pleaseth thee'.

..It is of great benefit in prayer to make petitions again and again, earnestly beseeching God with humility and confidence for his light, for pardon of sins, perseverance, a good death, Paradise and above all for the grace of divine love.

...Lastly the conclusion of Mental prayer is made up of three acts of thanksgiving to God for inspirations received, of purpose to observe exactly the resolutions made, of Petitions to the Eternal Father for the sake of Jesus and Mary, for help to continue faithful.Then finish by commending to God the souls in purgatory, the prelates of the Church, sinners and all relations and friends and benefactors by reciting an Our Father and a Hail Mary...." [10]

Another work of St Alphonsus for which Coffin provided a preface is entitled *The Mysteries, The Incarnation*

"..enter the cave of Bethlehem, approach the crib, and gaze on that Divine Child who is weeping, trembling and suffering the hardships of poverty and cold for thee.. If thou wouldst order well thy daily life, sanctify even the most ordinary actions and turn them into merits for eternity, perform the duties of thy state in the spirit of prayer and in union with God; bid St Alphonsus conduct thee to the cot of Nazareth, dwell there with the Holy Faily with Jesus, Mary and Joseph, watch well the actions of that young Boy, thy Redeemer and thy God, his obedience to Mary and to to Joseph, His profound humility, His divine simplicity.."

If that strikes the reader as rather simplistic in terms of the 20th century then a later passage still has lessons for us all.

"..another point suggested by Infancy of Our Lord

> which we will just touch upon is this. We live in an age of untiring activity in an age which measures success by immediate, visible and palpable results in which no sooner is a work begun than men are at once impatient to see its completion. The world cannot bear to work step by step to watch the proper place and time, and occasion for its designs, all must be done at once...Would we learn to be patient as God is patient, to order things as He does, sweetly to be content with the knowledge that when we have done our best, whether in the work of our own sanctification or in our efforts for the good and salvation of others, we must after all wait patiently and hope and pray, leaving the result to the good providence of God. [11]

There were other aspects to Fr Coffin's life at this time. For most of the period he was in command of the mission at Clapham. Yet this in itself presented a problem. Although parishes as such did not exist in England at the time, the missionary areas drawn up were in effect as much parishes as a modern day parish would be. However the rule of St.Alphonsus did not envisage the Fathers taking on parochial administration of large city parishes at all. The 1st Bishop of Southwark was well aware of this anomaly when he took control of his see in 1851 and to settle the matter canonically he appointed Fr Sheahan who had been acting as chaplain to the "Filles de Marie" to be in charge of Clapham so far as administration and parochial activities were concerned. He did not live in community but in a nearby house.

Luckily it presented no real problems and two years later Fr.Sheahan went off to the Crimea as a chaplain. Unfortunately he died of cholera out there. He was not replaced at once but in 1857 a Fr. Schofield was appointed and though he was doing good work and was much appreciated by Fr.Coffin, he became disillusioned with his anomalous position and retired to Birmingham. At that point the Bishop decided that the Fathers should have complete control and this was agreed with the provincialate. The final ruling on this matter came from

Rome and was communicated to the Fathers at Clapham by Bishop Grant. The Fathers were to exercise the care of souls in the Clapham Missionary District "ex solo titulo caritatis" with the obligation of observing all the precepts laid down in Provincial Synods. (15th Sept 1859).

Another local problem was that of the Church bells. When the Church was opened the peal of bells rang out loudly and the next door neighbour complained about the noise. He took the matter to court and the bells were ordered to remain silent. As soon as the bell hater died in 1864 Father Coffin lost no time in purchasing his house for the order and the bells rang out again on Christmas Day 1864.There has been no trouble there since!

Meanwhile the ordinary day to day troubles of a large Parish were always to hand. He wrote frequently to his Bishop, Thomas Grant of Southwark usually requesting permissions of one kind or another or dispensations. In 1857 for instance we find Coffin rather upset with the Christian Brothers who had recently opened a boys academy in the Parish.

Clapham, August 15th 1857

> "Is it prudent to say the least that the Christian Brothers should walk from their house to the Church and School with their habits and rabbas fully displayed ? This is their present custom and I am much afraid that it will lead to considerable annoyance. There is no doubt this is contrary to law and in Clapham it is especially most dangerous on account of the fanatical spirit which reigns here. May I suggest to them the necessity of doing as we do; in winter we tuck up our habits and hide our collars etc with a cloak. In Summer we always go out to the convents and elsewhere in our secular clothes."..[12]

Although Coffin is technically correct here in his attitude we might well compare this view with that of Blessed Dominic Barberi who always wore his religious attire even if it meant being pelted with stones at times.

One of his parishioners at Clapham was Richard Simpson, the subject of a later essay here. They generally enjoyed good relations.

Coffin wrote to Simpson in May 1856 after the publication in the *Rambler* magazine of two articles dealing with Original Sin. First Coffin told him the points that some theologians objected to and then concluded "If little people have begun to oppose I expect the great ones elsewhere will not remain quiet. I hope they will not, as I feel that the question is worth agitation. So good courage and be prepared to see yourself in the *Index* one of these days." [13]

In 1861 after the publication an article in the May number of the *Rambler* in which Simpson attacked the Church for what he called "police regulations" which fettered free exercise of the mind, Coffin wrote to Bishop Grant:

"It is hard for me to say what effect a letter from your Lordship would have on poor Simpson. If this is to do any good at all Your Lordship must make him feel that you write "proprio motu" owing to the views expressed in the *Rambler* especially in the May number of this year." [14]

The *Rambler* was censured by the hierarchy in 1862 and a certain Redemptorist, almost certainly Coffin, was not inclined to give Simpson absolution. The account given by Simpson in a letter to Lord Acton is both sad and amusing.

Easter Monday (21st April 1862)
"This morning the Redemptorist to whom I confessed asked me to call on him. It was the same story with a former Redemptorist. He could not hear my confessions after the Cardinal's address. I asked him what he wished me to do in order that he might be able to continue hearing me but I could not bring him to book....I saw there was always something behind which he would not bring out - of course a promise from me that I would write no more in the *Home and Foreign* - but when I plumply asked whether this was it, he disclaimed all right of such dictation.

I gave him to wit that he was a mere tool in the hands of a gigantic tyranny which wanted to force on us not

> only the dogmas and laws of the Church, but eke out its own 'instincts' and 'tones' and 'old womanisms', and that I should stand on my rights - That the Cardinal had not had the politeness to send me a copy of the writings denouncing me, that I had not bought it, and certainly should not, and should take no notice whatever of it till it was formally communicated to me. Finally I said that I was infamously treated etc, on which he went down on his knees-so to prevent his forthwith scourging himself I also went down on mine; assured him that my answer was no consequence of his personal clownishness, but that I should have answered anybody else in the same way. I finished by assuring him..that he personally enjoyed my highest consideration" [15]

It so happened that around this time the Clapham Fathers had to look after Richard Simpson's brother, Robert Simpson, priest of the diocese of Southwark who suffered from periodic brainstorms and had to abandon the active ministry. Richard was most grateful for the treatment accorded to his brother.

A fuller account of the difficulties over the *Rambler* and *Home and Foreign Review* will be given in the Chapter dealing with Richard Simpson.

In 1864 every mission in the diocese of Southwark had to send up to the Bishop a detailed account of the Mission and how it was organised.

The Clapham report is incomplete but contains some interesting sidelights on activities. The Parish covered a huge area including Battersea, Stockwell, and Brixton besides Clapham itself. Today the area is served by about eight missions besides Clapham St. Mary's.

Coffin said that he estimated there were 1400 Catholics in the area from a total population of between 20 and 30 thousand. The Church was open daily from 5.30am until 8.30pm on weekdays except for a lunchtime closure from 12 until 2.00pm. Confessions were available nearly all that time only ceasing after 6.30pm. The devotions used in the Church were the Stations of the Cross, once a month, weekly in Lent, the Exercise for a Happy Death; once a month, Devotions to the Infant Jesus, on the 25th of each month; and the Little Rosary of the Immaculate Conception every Saturday. The full Rosary was said every Wednesday and two Sundays each month.[16]

CHAPTER FIVE
Coffin and Manning.
He is elected Provincial.

Manning and Coffin had first met when Coffin was still an Anglican. Perhaps even on that occasion they had barely spoken as Coffin entrusted Miss Lockheart to ask Manning the question which Coffin wished to put regarding whether Anglicans who believed all the Catholic dogmas should remain in the Anglican Communion. It is possible that they might have met earlier but there is no record of this. They had in common the fact of both being ex Harrovians but Coffin was much younger.

They met up again in 1853 and Lubienski records that Coffin found Manning 'stuck up and cold' and that he did not make a good impression. A short while later after the publication of *The Mysteries - the Incarnation* they met up again by chance and Manning told Coffin "I have read something you have written and must have a good talk with you about it." The visit was fixed up but when Manning arrived, before Manning could introduce his topic, Coffin took him aside and told him flatly what he thought of him. "That he had the parson still in him, that he received converts too quickly without instructing them thoroughly - that he was stiff and cold"

Manning listened with humility to the younger man and told Coffin that he must promise one thing.."it is that for the glory of God, you will always speak out to me thus the truth".

The result of this conversation was a warm friendship between the two men and that Coffin became Manning's confessor. The future Cardinal always tried to come over to

Clapham to celebrate the Feast of St.Alphonsus. A further result of their friendship was that Coffin promoted the case for Manning's succession to Westminster when in Rome. Lubienski gives a full account of what happened [17]. In outline Coffin had been with the Provincial of the Order to an audience with Pius IX. He was introduced to the Holy Father and he asked him "who will become Archbishop now ?" Coffin replied that they spoke much about Mgr Errington. The Pope rose in anger and said that would be an insult to the Pope, then added "but it is to be Mgr.Clifford." Then he added as if he remembered something "But we must leave it to the Holy Spirit". Thinking that Clifford was already the Bishop chosen to succeed and considering him not entirely worthy of the position, Coffin informed the Provincial of his worries. He suggested Manning would be an ideal candidate. Cardinal Reisach was approached but the Provincial told him that only he the Cardinal could relay this important information to the Holy Father. Some time later Cardinal Reisach called and told Coffin how impressed the Holy Father had been with his narration.

At this point the account given by Pucell in his *Life of Cardinal Manning*, leaves out a very interesting piece of information. The full text taken from Lubienski's narrative reads,

"Cardinal Reisach related to him how the Holy Father had been very impressed with the narration and that his Holiness had added that if that were really so he must make Coffin Archbishop! Were these words of the Holy Father really serious and was there a question of his elevation? Father Coffin did not say another word to me (Lubienski) about this. He said only, treating it as a farce, that he replied to Cardinal Reisach, "That's only his little joke "

Once the Terna of the Canons had been received in Rome, nominating Errington and seeing that Grant and Clifford had stood down in his favour the Holy Father put aside the canons choice and took the nomination into his own hands. Although all the members of Propaganda whom he consulted were in favour of Ullathorne, the advice of Reisach prevailed and Manning was chosen.

Coffin had been in Rome at the time because the Provincial of the order had arranged a special meeting of Provincials and Vice Provincials to take place there. During the conference on the 24th of May, he was appointed the first full provincial of the newly constituted Province of England and Ireland. On his return he continued to reside at Clapham but henceforth gave very few retreats or missions. His work entailed a canonical visitation of each house every year to examine carefully the state of the house and each member. He was entitled to draw up a Code of Regulations for the better observance of Regular Discipline. So from time to time he issued circulars to the different houses. For instance in 1866 he wrote on "The Direction of Lay Novices" In the same year he offered a paper "On some defects in preaching". Between 1866 and 1869 he was much concerned with the setting up of the Remeptorist house at Kinnoul in Scotland. The new house was inaugurated on 19th March 1869. In the intervening years before he became Bishop he also established the house at Teignmouth in Devon as a house of studies and sanitorium for the sick. In that very house he would himself come to die.

He was re-elected regularly as the Provincial in spite of increasing ill health which meant that he had to spend increasing amounts of time taking cures at Spas like Aix La Chappelle or Harrogate. In 1881 he founded his final house at Dundalk in Ireland and travelled to Rome to conduct the necessary business regarding the foundation of a Mission at Singleton in Australia.

But what kind of administrator was he? The main accounts of his work are found in the Lubienski Memoir and the separate memoir prepared by Fr Bridgett. These are naturally enough entirely favourable to Fr. Coffin. However there is another side to the picture. In the book *Reapers of the Harvest - The Redemptorists in Great Britain and Ireland 1843 to 1898*, a slightly different picture emerges.The author, John Sharp, had access to a wide range of documents of the Redemptorist Fathers and a picture of Coffin as somewhat pernickety emerges.

Coffin wrote in 1864 (in the Lubienski Memoir)

> "We have few vocations, the Jesuits and communities without vows, the Oratorians and the Oblates of St Charles are in fashion... (this is due to.. the true state of the world in general which does not dispose souls to give up their liberty in the religious life; and in England in particular where the youth is accustomed to baths each morning, to physical exercises and to so many of life's comforts."

Examination of the Rome documents shows however that after his appointment as Provincial letters were received by the General about his manner of government, and that his position had been unassailable.

There had been a groundswell of opinion among a large number of his subjects that he had ruled despotically rather than authoritatively, often acting above the heads of local superiors, concentrating all decisions into his own hands, ruling through a chosen band of favourites mainly converts, employing a system of espionage, that he was ruthless in suppression of dissident voices, severe and unbending in the application of the Rule and Constitutions whilst lax himself in keeping them." [18]

The point about keeping of the rule is unfair to Coffin. After 1862 he was constantly ill with gout and/or bronchitis and so was quite unable to keep the full rigours of the rule.

Another allegation was that he was in effect anti-Irish in that he refused a second foundation there until very late and refused several postulants from Ireland. But against that it can be said that he had a very difficult task in trying to merge two very different temperaments.

It is perhaps sad to relate that particularly after Coffin had been made Vice Provincial for England, he clashed repeatedly with Fr. Lans, the priest who had encouraged him in his vocation while he was still an Oratorian. Sharp describes Fr Lans as "A man of great force of character of firm decision, of resolution, ardent courage, and practical energy which qualities brought him into conflict with Coffin at different times.". Indeed so, these were the very qualities that Coffin possessed. A personality clash was almost inevitable.

Yet while Coffin was obviously struggling to maintain the highest possible standards in the houses of the order and was perhaps over severe in dealing with faults, when it came to his own dealings with his superiors his actions bordered on servility. He wrote frequently to Rome almost in a grovelling mode. Shaw quotes one letter giving a good example of this servile approach.

> "...The least desire of your Paternity has always been for me like a formal order and long ago I made a firm resolution to place myself without question in obedience to your desires.." He also spoke of the General in terms reserved for the Pope. "To be with your paternity is to be allowed to look on the face of God's Vicar." It is also related that whenever he received a letter from Rome, he kissed it and placed it on his head, thereby submitting his will entirely to his Superior even before he knew his desire."[19]

CHAPTER SIX.
Appointed Bishop of Southwark. Death.

The 2nd Bishop of Southwark, James Danell died on the 14th June 1881. After a delay of nine months nearly every priest in Southwark and Coffin himself must have been astonished to hear that the Redemptorist Provincial had been appointed the 3rd Bishop. He was certainly not nominated by the Canons in their Terna so how did the choice come to be made.? According the Propaganda archives a letter was received in Rome purporting to come from several members of the Southwark clergy to the Cardinal at Propaganda Fidei. After listing the necessary qualities for a Bishop in England the letter expresses the view that Coffin satisfied the requirements and that he was almost a Bishop already in that he was the chief counsellor of all our Bishops and the intimate friend of the majority of them especially of his Eminence Cardinal Manning, and that he had the confidence of a good section of the Clergy.[20]

What is quite clear is that Manning had been pulling the strings again in Rome. Coffin was quite clearly Manning's personal nomination as a kind of reward for all his help. The long pause before the new Bishop was appointed occurred because Manning had used the opportunity of the vacancy at Southwark to have that diocese divided and the new diocese of Portsmouth created.

Manning also believed that he needed a more suppliant Bishop at Southwark because of the problems he faced from Danell over the question of funding the major orphanages in London.

Coffin lost no time in writing to Rome to reject the nomination. He may have been ambitious but certainly not for the episcopate. Anyway his health was so bad he could not manage the work load. He wrote also to every house in the province asking for prayers that he might be spared this onerous burden.

However the Holy Father would have none of it and he was confirmed in the post. He left England for Rome on the 18th May 1882 and was consecrated Bishop in the Church of St. Alphonsus by Cardinal Howard on June 11th. Returning to England in July he was installed on the 26th at St.George's Cathedral. Strangely he did not take up residence at Bishop's House but obtained for himself a property known as Brook House on Clapham Common backing on to the Redemptorist property. He took up residence here on August 19th accompanied by his secretary, Fr.Ford, two or three servants and a cat.

The Diocese he took over at that time covered the area now included under the diocese of Arundel and Brighton as well as Southwark itself. The area was increasing rapidly in population. More churches were needed to serve the growth of new suburbs. There was no Seminary and it was clear that this would be a pressing problem very soon as the numbers of Southwark students taken at St.Edmund's Ware was limited.

Poor Bishop Coffin must have felt overwhelmed. He was in poor health and knew comparatively few of the priests of the diocese personally.

In the event he had about two years of effective rule in front of him as most of the last year of his life was spent at Teignmouth.

A few major events however should be noted as taking place during his episcopate. One of the most important was the opening of the first Charterhouse in England since the reformation at Parkminster in Sussex, still happily going strong today. In his synod he clarified the role of the Dean and rearranged the deaneries.More importantly he started up a committee of temporal administration...that is to say what we would call today a Finance Committee. The committee acted as a check on the activities of the Diocesan Financial Chief, at that time always a layman with one priest advisor. As the diocese had just been divided and the division had operated most unfairly against the finances of Southwark, he felt the need for a proper committee to take more care of the interests of the Diocese. He was forced to sell a good site in Clapham itself which would have made an excellent Seminary.

The Bishop did whatever he could in the way of Visitations and Confirmations but he had no opportunity to make a complete round before ill health robbed him of the chance to complete the circuit.

Wisely he left the existing curial officers in their positions. The only major change in important posts was that of the Diocesan Inspector of Schools. This was Dr.Wenham, an old friend of Coffin's from Oxford days. He retired however shortly after Coffin became Bishop and a new appointment became necessary.

The Bishop only wrote about four full length pastoral letters before illness curtailed his activities and these together with the introductions to the translations of St Alphonsus' works are the only printed publications that he has left us. A few quotes from them however give us a picture of what his retreats and missions must have been like. One can almost hear Coffin delivering the words in person.

This first extract is from the Pastoral for Lent 1883:

> "St Thomas says that both the inernal and external sufferings of Jesus Christ exceeded all the pains which can be endured in this life.We know what He suffered in His blessed Soul; 'My Soul is sorrowful even unto death'. He suffered unspeakable pains and torments in all his senses; in His sense of touch, because all His flesh was torn by the scourging; in His taste, from the gall and vinegar; in His hearing, through the blasphemies and mockeries that were offered to Him; in His sight, at beholding His blessed Mother, who was present at His death. He suffered also in all the members of His Body. His head was tortured with thorns; His hands and feet with nails; His face with buffetting and spitting; and His entire body with scourging, so that He became, as it were a leper who had no sound portion in His body, and strikes horror into every one who sees him."

In October 1883 he wrote in his Pastoral about the importance of prayer in our spiritual lives:

> "We need hardly remind you Beloved Children, that at any moment, we are liable to temptations of various kinds; that our life here on earth is one perpetual struggle against the enemies of Salvation, and that these temptations for the most part assault us in the midst of the occupations of our daily life, in the times which elapse between Morning and Night Prayers, between Sunday and Sunday, between one Confession and Communion and another. Upon the victory over these temptations our perseverance in the service of God depends. This victory is hopeless without the ACTUAL grace of God, that is of Grace given at the very moment of temptation. This grace, we repeat is not given unless we ask for it, and therefore unless we pray we shall yield to the temptation and fall away from the service of God, and be in danger of everlasting ruin. It is this truth which gives meaning to the words of Our Divine Lord 'We must always pray and not faint'...Again and again in Holy Scriptures the necessity of continual prayer is urged upon us as the means of

overcoming all our spiritual difficulties, and of living in the service of God. The efficacy of Prayer rests not upon our own merits but on the faithfulness, the power and mercy of God...When you feel a struggle approaching between what your conscience tells you to be the will of God and the suggestions of your fallen nature, lift up at once without delay, your hearts to the good God, cry out and say to Him "O God come to my help, Lord save me I perish, My Jesus mercy, Mother of God pray for me, My Angel Guardian assist me, My Patron Saint help me."

The final extract is from the Pastoral for Advent 1882. This is particularly typical of a Redemptorist mission sermon of the period.

"He is waiting for us, knowing as He does our spiritual poverty, in order to enrich us with His graces, with His own Divine life and strength. He is waiting to give Himself to each one individually, that He may console us in the trials and difficulties of this life. He invites us to His own table and is Himself our Food; and yet how few there are who heed his invitation! Numbers are altogether spiritually deaf; they are so dead in sin and in spiritual sloth that they cannot hear His voice, whilst too many, as in the parable, know full well that the banquet is prepared, and that all things are ready, but excuse themselves and thus show that they have no real practical love of Our Lord Jesus Christ.....But beloved children, think you that these excuses will hold good when we stand at the dread tribunal of Christ, who then will not only be our Redeemer, but our Divine all - seeing Judge? Prepare yourself then dear Children, during these holy days of Advent, by prayer, examination of conscience, and by avoiding the wilful occasions of sin for a good, since and humble confession, so that at Christmas you may make a good and worthy Holy Communion..."

As a loyal son of St Alphonsus he always promoted devotion to Our Blessed Lady and had a particular devotion to the Holy Family at Bethlehem. He was also a firm supporter of Cardinal Manning's views on Temperance. In a Lenten pastoral for instance he recommended abstinence from alcohol as a substitution for abstinence from meat to those who were unable to comply with the precept of the Church.

In spite of the earlier criticisms made against him about not favouring the Irish, in his writings and sermons as a Bishop he showed a great sympathy for the Irish people, organising a collection for the relief of poverty in Ireland and in a St Patrick's Day sermon saying: "No means have been left untried to wrest from a down trodden race, the one precious gift that God Himself gave them, the gift of their Faith. Poverty, obscurity and oppression, have done their worst , yet today their Faith, and their love of God and Holy Church is stronger than ever !" [21]

In July 1884 his health broke down completely. Already in May his general condition had started to weaken and to an extent far greater than he was conscious of. He suffered much from bronchitis nevertheless he managed to keep all his engagements for a while.

In June he was able to confirm at St. George's Cathedral on Pentecost Sunday and on the 8th at Bermondsey. On the 11th he ordained a priest in his Private Chapel and on the 15th he confirmed at Brixton. He then fell ill but rose from his sick bed to go to the Diocesan Synod at St George's. During the remainder of the month he visited Roehampton , Caterham and Kingston.

In July he kept several engagements including the consecration of the Abbey at Ramsgate. However this act was too much for his declining strength . Two days later he preached and confirmed at Battersea but on his return he found he could barely ascend the steps to his House. Therefore the following day he set off for the Redemptorist House at Teignmouth.

He intended only to spend a month or two there but he did not improve in health but rather deteriorated faster. He was however able to keep up general administration by means of letters. There was a slight improvement in the new year but by then the Bishop knew he was dying. He petitioned the Holy Father for an auxiliary and nominated Canon John Butt, rector of Arundel as his candidate. Butt had been a chaplain in the Crimean War and had nearly died of fever out there.

He was consecrated on January 29th 1885 and succeeded to the see of Southwark at the death of Bishop Coffin.

After a brief period of improvement, Bishop Coffin's health declined still further and by Holy Week it was clear his end was at hand. By now he was unable to walk or stand. His mind remained clear and he died peacefully on Easter Monday April 6th 1895. It was six in the morning, and at that very hour his housekeeper at Clapham was amazed to see the Bishop sitting in his room. Before she could recover though he had promptly disappeared again !

By his own wish he was buried in the cemetery at Teignmouth and not at St George's Cathedral. The funeral and internment took place on the Thursday of the same week with Mass celebrated by Bishop Vaughan of Plymouth assisted by Bishop Clifford of Clifton. Both of these prelates had indeed been present at his reception into the Church many years before. Bishop Butt, the auxiliary of Southwark came down for the ceremony which was attended by about 30 local priests. The main Requiem took place the following Monday when Bishop Weathers, auxiliary in Westminster celebrated Mass in the presence of Cardinal Manning, eight other Bishops and over 300 priests and religious.

A few days later a special Mass was celebrated at St Mary's Clapham at which Fr. Bridgett gave the address. This sermon has come down to us luckily in printed form. It is certainly a magnificent eulogy of his old friend. In it he outlined the Bishop's life and then outlined his virtues as a priest. We learn for instance that his favourite reading in his last years was Butler's Lives of the Saints. The Bishop kept his judgement free and healthy as to historic facts and according to Bridgett his enjoyment of Butler's pages was derived from two sources. "They present a magnificent panorama of God's marvellous dealings with the human soul in all times and countries and the history is recorded with a learned humility and a piety that is transparently sincere. Butler was too sincere to put down anything he did not believe to be historically true, and at the same time too sincere to suppress from fear of criticism anything however extraordinary or marvellous that has com down to us on trustworthy evidence." Bridgett relates several anecdotes and stories of the late Bishop:

> "One of the comic papers had published a cartoon in which the Pope was represented in some unseemly guise. The intention of the artist had not been to cast ridicule on the Sovereign Pontiff but on the contrary the laugh was on some statesman who was his opponent.....Father Coffin entered the room and the cartoon was handed to him. I shall never forget the holy anger with which he glanced at it for a second and then tore it to pieces and the sterness of the rebuke he gave...he said it was next to sacrilege and blasphemy thus to caricature the living representative of the King of Kings...No the thing is abominable and I forbid such pictures ever again to be brought into this house."

Bridgett too relates somehing of his last few moments on earth:

> "...he had few temptations. He often used to remark calmly and lovingly 'Oh, how strange, how terrible, how joyful a thing to come suddenly into the presence of the Incarnate God.'..."

Just before he death, his confessor heard him say something incoherent and feared he was in trouble. ' Are you tempted my Lord?', he said. 'No, not a bit' was the prompt reply; and so with a prayer on his lips, with a strange light in his upturned gaze, his soul passed from his body" Bridgett is also very generous to Coffin in his memoir. Again he relates several stories and anecdotes. On one occasion he took up residence for a week with his friend and great benefactor at Clapham, Sir John Lambert. His son was dying and he helped care for the lad during the last days of his life so that his parents could get some rest. Once he had to stand perfectly still for over an hour as the lad had fallen asleep while holding his hand and she did not wish to move for fear of rousing the sleeping patient. Yet all the while Coffin was nearly writhing in pain from an acute attack of sciatica.

We are told that Coffin was not a great orator for he was somewhat "lacking in the imaginative faculties." This was compensated for by the "copiousness of his Scriptural Knowledge and the clearness of his Expositions."

Bridgett says" that he had a nice sense of humour and was quick in detecting human foibles which no feeling of human respect prevented him from playfully alluding to before the face rather than behind the back of anyone subject to them." However such behaviour in a superior could also be taken as a rebuke and the only incident relating anything like a sense of humour was the fact that on a long train journey if he wished to be alone and someone tried to enter the carriage at a station he would lean out and say " I think you ought to know that there is a Coffin in here" and the person would usually move further down the platform!

It should be clear enough from this account of Coffin's life to see why Coffin was as it were "on the same wavelength" as Cardinal Manning. They both had a very exalted view of the Papacy and all that the Holy Father did. So inevitably they both supported Papal Infallibility and the importance of loyalty to the Holy See.

Coffin too had learnt the important lesson of spiritual simplicity and could bear no criticism whatever of those in authority. His own faith was moulded on that of St. Alphonsus...devotion to Our Lady, the importance of the Passion and Death of Christ, the need for sinners to convert before they died. He was particularly devoted to the Holy Family and used the Christmas Story frequently in his sermons. His general aim in life was to seek perfection not just in himself but in others and so at times he could seem very strict and overbearing.

He was on the other hand extemely devoted to the sick and the dying at times making long journeys just to be with a sick confrere.

On the negative side he became increasingly narrow minded and anti-intellectual as time went by. As mentioned earlier at one time he supported Simpson and his *Rambler* articles but later he opposed the entry of Catholic Youth to Oxford and Cambridge as strongly as Manning nor would he have any truck with the idea of a Catholic College at Oxford. He was asked twice to give his views on University Education.

His replies are contained in the Coffin papers at Southwark.

On the first occasion about 1868 he writes.

> "I should consider it a grievous sin to expose unnecessarily even a talented young Catholic and far more one of only moderate abilities, to the attractive influence naturally speaking of such men as Professor Jowett and Dean Stanley."

In the same reply he writes scathingly of the Oxford system.

> "...It is still as it ever has been since the Reformation the Seminary and hotbed of Anglicanism,of Church of England orthodoxy, and Evangelicalism; the stronghold and perpetual propagator of the Elizabethan tradition and the school of false nationality, and of the absurd and narrowminded spirit which pretends to despise and deprecate everthing that is not English. It is at Oxford that a man learns to perfection 'the gentleman's heresy' and with it the adoration of national greatness and prosperity, of success or rank and wealth, and social position, and of all that the world prizes...indeed I know of no place where nature is seen to counterfeit grace more exquisitely as Oxford as it was in my time and for this reason especially do I consider it so dangerous for the children of the faith."

Finally he writes

> "...should a considerable body of young Catholics finish their education in Oxford or Cambridge the result would be the formation of a future Catholic body *less* conscientious,

> less orthodox, less religious, less devout, less pure than we can obtain by keeping the education of our youth as far as possible in our own hands."

In 1882 when asked again about the admission of youths to Oxford he wrote

> "The light which was mercifully granted to me now 38 years since, has shown to me that the National Universities are not and cannot be places of higher education for Catholic Youths.....That it is wrong in principle and contrary to the teaching of the late Pope Pius IX, that it is most dangerous to the faith and the Catholic Spirit."

One must surely regret that the Oxford College for Catholics proposed by Newman came to nothing. The attitude shown here by Coffin and shared by nearly all the hierarchy was obscurantist. Surely if a young man had been given a good education first of all, then his faith should have been sufficient to withstand any possible temptation at University especially with the protection of a Catholic College? Of course in time such views prevailed but it always seems surprising that the very men like Manning and Coffin who had received a University Education and yet been later received into the Church could not appreciate what it had done for them.

The final word on Bishop Coffin though should be left to Fr. Bridgett CSSR who concludes his memoir with these words:

> "We cannot fail to be impressed with the conviction that there was one sentiment that pervaded his whole life and that may I think be well described by the single word DUTY."

NOTES AND SOURCES

As indicated at the start of this essay, the main sources for the life of Robert Coffin are the Lubienski Manuscript Life and the separate memoir prepared (probably) by Father Bridgett. Both these are kept in the Clapham Provincial Archives of the English Redemptorist order. The Lubienski document is in French but a translation of about half the material has been provided by an anonymous person.

The Clapham archives also contain some personal letters, the very sad correspondence between himself and John Henry Newman, and many documents concerning the running of the order.

The Southwark Diocesan Archives contain his letters while Bishop, his diaries while Bishop, his pastorals and Ad Clera, his report of 1864 on the condition of the Clapham Mission and finally his Will.

Notes

1) Lubienski states that Coffin was confirmed by Charles Sumner Bishop of Chichester. In fact Sumner was Bishop of Winchester at the time.
2) For a good account of the opening of St. George's Cathedral see *The Great Link* by Bernard Bogan, (London 1948) pages 128ff.
3) A detailed account of these moves amonst the Oratorians is given in Meriol Trevor's work *The Pillar of the Cloud* London 1962 and also in the *Letters and Diaries* of John Henry Newman Vol XIV
4) *Letters and Diaries* Vol XIV page 88. Oct 3rd. Fr Nicholas brings.a letter from Coffin to Newman
5) *Letters and Diaries* Vol XIV Newman's reply also Oct 3rd. Page 88
6) *Letters and Diaries.* Vol XIV pages 137 and 139 (21st Nov)
7) *Letters and Diaries* Vol XIV. Stanton relays to Faber the information about Baron Von Schroeter (Letter Nov 26th). Lubienski makes no reference whatever to the Baron.
8) For the life of St.Alphonsus see. St. Alphonsus own

autobiography. Life of St. Alphonsus by Fr Austin Berthe, Dublin 1906 and other standard biographies..

9) For a detailed account see Stebbing. History of St. Mary's Clapham, London, 1935

10) Introduction to *Preparation for Death*..This work was translated in 1844 but not by Coffin. His translation relates to the 1855 edition.

11) Introduction to *The Mysteries of the Faith.The Incarnation*, London 1854. The book is one of a series of St.Alphonsus works translated by Fr. Coffin.

12) Southwark Archives (SAA) Coffin Papers.

13) *Richard Simpson 1820-1876* by Damian McElrath. Louvain 1972. The reference is Page 59.

14) S.A.A. Coffin Papers

15) Simpson to Acton quoted by McElrath,(op.cit) 3rd Sept 1862 page 88

16) S.A.A. The 1864 Visitation Returns Box.

17) Also in Purcell's Life of Cardinal Manning.

18) Sharp. *Reapers of the Harvest* p48.

19) Sharp. op.cit.p 38

20) Sharp. op. cit. p.45

21) S.A.A. Pastorals and Ad Clera (Coffin).

PART TWO
Frederick Oakeley
Always in Newman's Prayers

Introduction

The Second of this quintet of Converts was one of the most important members of the Oxford Movement to become a Catholic. Today he is almost entirely forgotten although both as an Anglican and a Catholic he wrote many articles, pamphlets and books. The account here will give as much biographical information as possible as no full length study of his life has yet been published.

The earlier part of his life is better documented than the latter. He himself wrote a partial auto-biography which exists only in MSS in the library at Balliol College. He also contributed an autobigraphical sketch to *The Month* magazine in 1865 whichwas later reprinted in the *Reminiscences of Oxford and Oxford Men*, vol 22.

For the Oxford Movement he produced two pamphlets which outline his own part in the events of the time. He warrants a mention in all the standard work on the Oxford Movement because of his close association with both Newman and W.G. Ward and because of his activities in London at the Margaret Chapel.

His life as a Catholic was quieter. He wrote many books and gave many talks but the greater part of his work was the simple task of being the Rector of St John the Evangelist Church, Duncan Terrace, Islington for 30 years until his death.

The title for this part of the work owes its origin to the fact that we know that Cardinal Newman always kept Oakeley in his prayers. His name is still to be found in a list on Newman's desk at the Oratory of those he wished to remember in his prayers regularly.

He deserves to be better known and therefore I have included a fair number of quotations from his writings.

CHAPTER ONE. *Early Life.*

Frederick Oakeley was the youngest son of Sir Charles Oakeley, Governor of Madras from 1790 until 1795. While serving in India he had met and married Helena Beatson of Killerie in Fifeshire. They married in Madras in 1777 and had 14 children of whom 3 died in infancy. There were 8 sons and 6 daughters in all.

Sir Charles was a member of the younger branch of the Oakeley family from Oakeley in Shropshire. He settled his family in Shrewsbury and Frederick was born there on the 5th February 1802.

In his MSS autobiography at Balliol he recounts in some detail what he remembered of his earliest years. He recalls how he used to like the wall of the old Abbey and peep through an aperture to watch the arrival of the London Mail coach. His earliest memories were the commemmoration of the Victory of Trafalgar in 1805. In particular he remembered the sound of the bells and how in later life he was always much affected by the sound of bells. His father had been made colonel of the Shrewsbury Corps and he enjoyed playing with a drum kit and singing military songs.

He tells of an antipathy to frogs which he retained all his life and that if he was a bad boy he was told that "Boney was coming".

During the Napoleonic wars there had been a risk of invasion by Napoleon so this was a good way of frightening children.

From birth he had a weak ankle and in 1806 he fell on a slippery slope and broke his right thigh. The bone was set none too well it seems, without any anaesthetic, and it took a very long time for him to recover. It left him lame for the rest of his life. He had to spend long periods either in bed or seated. He used this time to learn to the play the piano and commit to memory long passages of Shakespeare as he was very fond of drama. By 1808 he was able to walk again and was taken to the local theatre which much impressed him. At this point in his narrative he adds a special footnote.

> " Here I cannot help remarking how important it is to give a right direction to what may be called the dramatic susceptibilities of youth.
> This duty is well understood by the Holy Catholic and Roman Church.
> That wise and loving mother by means of expressive symbolism of her ceremonial and attractive beauty of her processions, succeeds in winning to her side the interest and affection of her children who under a less considerate training might have been led to waste on pantomines and Lord Mayor's shows, the early cravings of an instinct implanted in our nature for a noble end."

In 1812 the family moved to the Episcopal Palace at Lichfield.

The Bishops at that time preferred to live out of town and let out their residence. Young Oakeley enjoyed the ritual of the Cathedral services which he described as "romantic". Up to this time he had been educated by his parents and just as they were considering what school to send him to he developed a very severe lumbar abscess which settled on his weak thigh. The problems that this caused lasted for up to 2 years but in 1814 his parents thought him well enough to attend Lichfield Grammar School as a day pupil. Oakeley tells that he was a solitary and lonely figure at school as he was unable to play with the other children. He did not have to spend long there as he developed another abcess and had to be educated again at Home unti 1817. [1]

At this point it may be useful to give some of Oakeley's reminiscences of Caholicity at Lichfield which he penned much later on. First of all comes the following extract from his 1865 book on the Trctarian movement.

> "I thought that the Roman Catholics of England did not at the most number more than 80 to 100 souls who were distributed in certain great families over the midland and northern counties. I thought that each of these families

lived in a large haunted house embosomed in yew trees and surrounded by high brick walls. About the interior of thee mansions I had also my ideas. I thought that they were made up of vast dreary apartments, walled with tapestry; with state bedrooms, in which were enormous beds with ebony bedsteads, surmounted by plumes, and which only required horses to be put to them in order to become funeral cars. I fancied of course, that there reigned around and within these abodes a preternatural silence, broken only by the flapping of bats and the screeching of owls."

He also gives his early view of Catholic priests based largely on Dr.John Kirk of Lichfield, well known Catholic author and historian who lived there for 50 years.

"I knew only that they had their little suburban chapels in which they perpetrated ineffable rites. The only token of humanity about them was of a rather pleasing character. It was the little modest presbytery by the side of the chapel......but who and what were the inmates of these dwellings? That they must be mortal was evident; but how did they employ themselves? They were never seen to be in public places, and if they ever went abroad it must be in company with the aforesaid owls and bats and other such shy and lucifugous creatures. Surely that could not be one of them whom we saw the other day working in his garden like a common labourer or coming out of that poor little cottage, so meanly clad, with his hand on his breast and his eyes on the ground ? Of course not, for priests are always represented in pictures and on the stage as big men, with haughty looks and shaven crowns."

Another similar account is to be found is Oakeley's pamphlet *The Catholic Church before and after Conversion* delivered as a lecture in 1855 and later printed.

"..I must dig deep into the caverns of my memory for my primitive ideas of the Catholic religion; and a very curious collection of fossil remains you will pronounce them! In the lowest stratum of all, I find an antediluvian specimen in the form of good old Dr Kirk of Lichfield though I much doubt if you will recognise his likeness in the shape in which I am about to present him. Many of you are probably aware that Dr. Kirk was a very model of an old priest; simple innocent devouot and learned; I have been labouring hard to recollect how he appeared to me when I was a boy and I think that the best idea I can give you is by asking you to fancy a sort of compound between a Jew Pedlar and a quack doctor. No one would tell me anything about him except that he was the "Catholic Priest" and what the "Catholic Priest" might be I thought it safest not to investigate.

The little chapel half a mile out of Lichfield on the London road in which unmentionable rites were perpetrated I used to look upon with supreme contempt by the side of the stately cathedral with which my early ideas of religion were associated; little thinking that in course of years I should come to pass that cathedral with a sigh while on my way to say Mass in that obscure little chapel" My next idea of the Catholic Church I think was derived from a school companion who was from Ireland and told me that he had often been into the Catholic Chapels in Dublin. I asked him what they did there and he replied 'nothing but sing Per omnia saecula saeculorum'......The nursery too contributed a powerful influence to support what Dr. Newman calls the great protestant tradition. 'The House that Jack built' impressed upon the infantine imagination an idea which still haunts me.

The Priest all shaven and shorn,
That married the man all tattered and torn
That wooed the maiden all forlorn."

Returning to the main account of his life we reach the year 1817 and he is sent off to a private tutor to prepare for Oxford. This tutor was Rev. Charles Sumner, later to become Bishop of Winchester. Sumner was a very interesting character. The Warwickshire Sumners of which he was a member had at one time been staunchly Catholic but Charles and his brother John were born when the family was equally staunchly Protestant. He studied at Eton where he contrived to write a sensational novel entitled "The White Nun, or The Black Bog of Dromore" This was published as being by "A Gentleman of Note". It soon became known that Sumner was the author as NOTE is ETON reversed. After graduating in 1814 he took orders in 1817. In 1821 he met with King George IV at Brighton and spoke with him for some three hours. This meeting led to quick preferment and in 1826 was appointed Bishop of Llandaff and the following year promoted to the see of Winchester aged only 37. In 1829 he lost the favour of the King as he voted in favour of Catholic Emancipation. He was a noted Evangelical and his brother John Bird Sumner became Archbishop of Canterbury.[2]

At the time Oakeley was his pupil, Sumner was Rector of Highclere. A fellow pupil was Lord Albert Conyngham. In the *Life of Charles Richard Sumner* Oakeley gives an interesting portrait a a typical day with a parson tutor. This extract from page 42 is from a letter that Oakeley wrote to the son of the Bishop in preparation for the biography.

> "We went into your father's study at 8 in the morning to construe a portion of the Greek Testament, and of some Greek play. We breakfasted at nine after family prayers, and after breakfast had half an hours recreation. We then went to our rooms till twelve when we met again in the study. We had a good portion of the afternoon to ourselves, dined at four and at seven in the evening carried up verses or other compositions to be corrected. When the evening exercise was finished we met for tea in the drawing room, after which your father used to read aloud one of Shakespeare's plays, portions of 'Childe Harold' and articles in the 'Quarterly' or some other standard work or publication of the day. At ten o'clock wc rctired to our rooms"

Oakeley relates an interesting anecdote about Sumner's sermons:

> "During a Greek New Testament lesson, I once contended with somewhat unbecoming vehemence, that Our Lord gave the keys of His Kingdom in an especial manner to St. Peter. My tutor, whose thoughts were at the moment on another text, and who might have instinctively feared that my argument had a dangerous tendency, maintained that the promise was given to all the Apostles alike. But he was far too

> honest to shrink from acknowledging the mistake from the fear of compromising his tutuorial dignity, and when we met the next morning he said to me: "I think, Oakeley, that you were right about St.Peter." I have often thought of this little incident as if there were something prophetic about it, though as far as I myself was concerned, I can truly say that I was most profoundly ignorant of any theological import in the remark."

Oakeley was, he relates, very happy during his stay with Sumner except for the first few weeks when he was bullied somewhat, but as the boys came to know him better, this unruly tendency died out.

He recovered his health and was able to walk several miles a day without difficulty. He enjoyed the local countryside "with its magnificent park, gently sloping hills, densely shaded pine woods, its glassy lakes and hedges of rhodedendrons."

After he moved on to Oxford he returned frequently to see Sumner in whatever position and locality he was placed in including Winchester.

However Oakeley relates he became shy of seeing him when at the Margaret Chapel and they did not meet after 1843. They did however correspond and the letters were kind and affectionate. Indeed at this point it may be worth pointing out that almost alone of all the Oxford converts, Oakeley was able to maintain friendly relations with every one of the important figures of the day that he had met in his Anglican period. Thus he was on good terms with both Manning and Newman, except for the few years before Manning became Cardinal. He knew Gladstone well and the great man would call on him at Islington. He remained on friendly terms with Sumner who in his years at Winchester was decidedly anti- Catholic in approach, and with Tait, later Archbishop of Canterbury. The ability to make friends and keep them is one of his endearing characteristics. Oakeley went on to Oxford to matriculate in 1820. He entered Christchurch College and relates that for the first term he was bundled about from one set of rooms to another and at length to his great joy sent home for lack of a place where to lay his head. He tells us that during those first few weeks, he conceived a disgust of college life which he never wholly conquered till after he had taken his degree. Amongst his fellow undergraduates at the time was the well known Dr. Pusey but Oakeley did not meet him at that time. Several members of the aristocracy were around of whom the most important was Athony Ashley Cooper (BA 1823) 7th Earl of Shaftesbury, the great reformer. Among the tutorial staff was Charles Longley, later head of Harrow while Coffin was there and later still Archbishop of Canterbury. His own tutor was John Bull, college proctor in 1820 and very eccentric, yet able to instil a love of classics into his pupils. Oakeley had two patrons at Oxford to whom he had introductions from his brother. One was Thomas Gaisford, distinguished Greek scholar and the other Philip Shuttleworth, fellow of New College and later Bishop of Chichester. It was Shuttleworth who encouraged Manning to take an active part in public life.

To start with all was not sweeetness and light at Oxford. Oakeley drifted into bad company and though he soon decided to have quit of them the result was that he then belonged to no particular set for the remainder of his undergraduate years. He was very disappointed when at the end of his undergraduate studies he only received a 2nd when he expected a 1st class degree. His father it seems was even more upset and so Oakeley resolved to return to the University to try for a fellowship. He had also by now determined to take orders. He did not think much of his colleagues at Christchurch at the time he was there.

Writing in *The Month* he says "I cannot recollect any set of men however regular in ordinary college duties and however given to reading, of whom I do not feel sure that....they were as a set addicted to vice and loose conversation." He considered though that by the time he left there had been a vast improvement, but his experiences at Christchurch apparently soured him against Oxford and he wrote that "my early impressions of Oxford were so exceedingly the reverse of pleasant that I could never wholly conquer them and I left with but little regret a place which I entered with the most glowing anticipations of happiness."

On his return to Oxford to prepare for the ministry and aim at a fellowship he at last joined his first club of friends. His coterie included Philip Henry, fifth Earl of Stanhope, and William Courtenay, 12th Earl of Devon. To gain prestige he entered the Chancellor's competition prize for a Latin Essay and duly won. The entitled him to read the prize winning essay in public at the Sheldonian. Later he also gained the Ellerton Prize for a theological essay. The topic was as follows.; "What was the object of the Reformers in maintaining the proposition and by what arguments did they establish it? i.e. 'Holy Scripture is the only sure foundation of an Article of Faith'"

Armed with these new credentials he joined a collection of 12 Oxford BA's who were trying to win two vacant fellowships at Oriel.

However they were awarded to Richard Hurrell Froude and Robert Wilberforce. The following year he tried again for one of the two vacancies at Balliol and this time lost out to Frank Newman and George Moberly. Not to be dismayed he asked to be admitted to orders and on succssive days was ordained Deacon and Priest by Charles Sumner.

This enabled him to apply for a Chaplain Fellowship. There was less competition for such posts and he was duly appointed Chaplain Fellow of Balliol in the autumn of the same year 1837.[3]

Tom Mozley describes Oakeley at this time in his *Reminiscenses:*

> "An elegant rather dilettante scholar, translating Lucretius into English verse, much at his piano, avowedly sentimental rather than decisive in his religious views, he seemed in a fair way to settle into a very common type of English

way to settle into a very common type of English Churchman."

That in the event was very far from what happened to Oakeley.

CHAPTER TWO. *At Oxford 1827-1839*

For the next twelve years or so Oakeley continued to reside at Oxford. These were momentous years at the University with the coming of the Oxford Movement and the growing importance of John Henry Newman particularly as Rector of St.Mary's.

The bare outline of Oakeley's life can be told in a few words.

In 1830 he became a tutor at Balliol. In 1831 he became a Select Preacher at Oxford and a Prebend at Lichfield Cathedral. In 1835 he became a public Examiner for the University and from 1837 until 1839 he was the Whitehall preacher for Oxford University.

Behind these bare facts lay a much more interesting life at the University including a strong involvement with the Oxford Movement.

From 1826 until 1828 Oakeley attended the special private lectures of Dr Charles Lloyd, regius professor of Divinity at Oxford. In 1827 he became the Bishop of Oxford but after voting in favour of Catholic Emancipation in 1829 he was spurned by his former colleagues. Never in the best of health he died soon afterwards from a chill caught after attending a dinner in London. His private lectures were attended only by special invitation and there has been much debate over the years as to whether they contributed in any way to the birth of the Oxford Movement. An interesting article by Donald Withey in the *Downside Review*, October 1993, entitled "John Henry Newman and Dr. Charles Lloyd" deals with this very point.

Newman only attended the first series of talks and did not attend any talks after 1826 at the very time Oakeley started coming to them.

However it was this second series attended by Oakeley and also by Hurrell Froude, Pusey and Robert Wilberforce that had a real bearing on the Oxford Movement. Only Pusey had attended the first series. Oakeley describes the lectures as "of a free and colloquial character where the lecturer converses rather than dogmatises and the pupils feel themselves at liberty to propose to him as many difficulties as he is benevolent enough to receive." "He never sat but instructed perpipatetically making the circuit of his class once and again...His treatment of his pupils was familiar and free to an extent upon which few men but himself could have ventured." The Dictionary of National Biography sketch of Lloyd suggests that in his private lectures Lloyd taught that the Book of Common Prayer was the reflection of medieval and primitive devotion still embodied in the Latin form in Roman text books." Indeed Lloyd introduced his students to missals and breviaries and this novelty proved so popular that they were sold even in Oxford itself.

But how was it that Lloyd came to develop an interest in such matters which had not been dealt with before by Anglican divines?

The answer would seem to lie in the fact that as a young newly ordained minister he worked for some time in London with French Emigré priests. When speaking in the House of Lords in the debate on Catholic Emancipation he recalled how he had become familiar with the Roman rite and spent much time in the company of a couple of Gallican priests. However he went on to say that he supported Catholic Emancipation not on the grounds of theological empathy but on grounds of charity. [4] Whatever the influence on John Henry Newman there was no doubt that the lectures had a great influence on both Froude and Oakeley. Froude reacted with great enthusiasm to Lloyd's treatment of the liturgy. This led eventually to his writing Tract 63. *The Antiquity of the Existing Liturgies* (1st May 1835) and in a general way to his best known work *Remains* published after his death in 1836.

Oakeley gives this account of the lectures in his "Historical Notes on the Tractarian Movement". This work was published in 1865 and is fuller than the accounts given in his own essay included in *The Month* or his *Personal Reminiscenses of the Oxford Movement* published in 1855. The following extract is from the 1865 work, (page 12)

"On the more proximate causes..I am disposed to give a very prominent place to the teaching of Dr. Charles Lloyd, Regius Professor of Divinity and afterwards Bishop of Oxford who died in 1829 about four years before the publication of 'Tracts for the Times'....The class of pupils assembled between the years 1826 and 1828 comprehended all the leading members of the great Tractarian movement with the exception of Dr. Keble who had then left the University. I was myself one of that class though somewhat junior in standing to Dr. Pusey and Mr Newman and....among other matters which Dr. Lloyd read and discussed with his class was the history of the Council of Trent and the use of the Anglican Prayer Book. There were of course two ways of treating both these subjects but Dr. Lloyd chose the more correct and Catholic one. I have no doubt whatever that his teaching had a most important influence upon the movement and - a point to which to I wish to draw particular attention - upon that movement in its ultimate and as I may call it - Roman stage. Upon the subjects of Church authority, Episcopacy, the Apostolical succession and others with which the earlier Tracts were almost exclusively occupied, I do not remember to have received very definite ideas from Dr. Lloyd's teaching but I do remember to have received from him an entirely new notion of Catholics and Catholic Doctrine. The fact was that Dr. Lloyd besides being a man of independent thought considerably in advance of the High Churchmen of his time, had enjoyed in his youth many opportunities of intercourse with the French emigrant clergy to whom he was indebted as he told us for truer views of the Catholic religion than were generally current in this country. In his lectures on the Anglican Prayer Book, he made us first acquainted with the missal and breviary as the sources from which all that is best and noblest in that compilation is derived...."

Oakeley went on to describe the sad events which terminated in his early death. In 1829 he spoke in support of the bill introducing Catholic Emancipation. This bill had initiated by the government led by the Duke of Wellington assisted by Sir Robert Peel. It was known that Dr Lloyd owed his episcopal see to the friendly intervention of Peel and now men at Oxford were imputing unworthy motives for the Bishop's change of heart on this matter as they saw it. Oakeley describes how Lloyd sent for him the day after he made a speech in the Lords defending his action. He indicates that he considered that even then Lloyd was suffering the symptons of the fever which would carry him off only six weeks later. He writes

> "The sad interval was full of events calculated to aggravate the malady. The week after his parliamentary display he appeared at the levee where King George IV who regarded the support of Catholic Emancipation as a personal insult, treated him with pointed rudeness. What he regarded as a far greater mortification than the rebut he had experienced from a capricious monarch was that at his visitation which followed soon after, the great body of his own clergy refused his invitation to dinner. Vexed and bitterly disappointed he took to his bed and a few days later expired..a victim as we may hope of his zeal in the cause of charity and justice." [5]

Whatever the overall effect of Lloyd's lectures on Newman were they certainly had a great influence on Oakeley and many of the principles of Lloyd are to be found in his later writings. However he was too busy at that time to write much except sermons. The Tractarian movement had not yet started. From 1830 until 1837 his main work was as a tutor at Balliol. One of his first subjects was Archibald Campbell Tait. Born in Edinburgh in December 1811 he was evidently a very bright scholar. He entered the newly formed Glasgow University at the age of 15 and determined on a career in the ministry of the Church of England. In 1829 he competed for a exhibition to Balliol, and matriculated there on 29th January 1830. Oakeley had helped him from the moment of his arrival and became his tutor. He graduated with a first in classics and became a fellow in 1834. He remained a good friend of

Oakeley's all his life ever remembering the help he had received in his early days at Oxford. Although their theological views differed considerably, Tait never doubted the piety of those who were conducting the Oxford movement. He later became head of Rugby School after Dr. Arnold, then Bishop of London in 1856 and finally succeeded Longley as Archbishop of Canterbury in 1869. He died in 1882.

At this time Oakeley was a close follower of Dr. Pusey. Liddon in his *Life* of Pusey states that Oakeley was one of the five committee members of Pusey's Theological Society along with Keble and Newman.

The members of the society fed the *British Critic* and the Tracts with a series of essays on subjects on which little was known or thought about in those days. Liddon considered that the Society stimulated theological thought and work more than any other agency in Oxford.

Oakeley is recorded as reading a paper on "The Rise and Progress of Jansenism" and assisting Pusey in the work of translating the Fathers of the Church. He started work on St Augustine's anti-Pelagian treatises.

Oakeley recalls that the debates in the Common Room at Balliol were fairly fierce but that he preferred not to enter controversy unless it became absolutely necessary. The common room must have become even more lively after the arrival on the scene of a new fellow, W.G. Ward in 1834. Although completely different in character, they shared the same theological outlook. Tom Mozley described their friendship as "As much associated as Damon and Pythias, Castor and Pollox or any other inseparable pairs." Their real work together though dates from around 1838. [6]

The work of tutoring was not really to Oakeley's taste but he needed the income it provided. In 1837 though,he was enabled thanks largely to Newman, to escape from this dreaded chore. He was appointed the Whitehall preacher for Oxford. At the end of 1836 Dr Blomfield, Bishop of

London had been looking around for someone from Oxford to fill the post of special preacher at the Whitehall chapel which had just been re-opened. He consulted Pusey first of all. Pusey then consulted Newman who wrote a long letter back giving names. Then he added "Oakeley is the safest card". The letter was sent on January 10th [7]

On 11th February 1837 Oakeley must have been very pleased indeed to receive the following communication from Dr.Blomfield. (The original of this letter somehow ended up in the Southwark Archives).

London House
11th Feb 1837.

Dear Sir,

The time is now come, when I must appoint two Preachers for Whitehall Chapel, which is about to be re-opened; one from each University; and it would give me much satisfaction should you be able and willing to accept the Oxford Preachership. The salary of each preacher will be £320.00 per annum; and I wish the office to be held for two years. The duty required of the Preachers (two Sermons each Sunday) might be arranged between them to suit their convenience. There will be no weekly duty of any kind, except on Christmas Day and I believe on Good Friday, so that the office may be held by a person residing in Oxford or Cambridge.

P.S. The Preacher will not have to read any part of the Church Service except the Communion Service. The Chapel will be opened on Easter Sunday."

signed C.J. London.

Oakeley printed his sermons after his two year stint was ended and sent a copy to Sir Robert Peel who it seems had listened to a few of these words of wisdom. Peel thanked Oakeley saying he was glad to accept a copy though he never heard a word of them and would be glad to acquaint himself with them.[8] Dozing off during sermons is no new phenomenom. A more critical response was that of Bishop Blomfield who was most displeased to find strong evidence of Tractarian sympathies in the text of the sermons. It is not however clear from the text of Oakeley' autobigraphical MS whether Blomfield had read them *before* granting a license to Oakeley to officiate at the Margaret Chapel in 1839. Surely if he had read them he might well have refused a license. During his time as the Whitehall preacher Oakeley had continued to reside at Balliol and was much involved in the development of the Oxford Movement under the influence of W.G. Ward in particular. The scene in the Common Room is described by Wilfred Ward in his work on W.G.Ward and the Oxford Movement. It was Ward in particular who persuaded Oakeley to take a more active role in the affairs and to side with him in giving the movement a new direction. The two of them were in constant debate with Tait. Luckily affairs never got out of hand and Ward and Tait remained friends after Ward became a Catholic.

Ward was the leader. Wilfred writes "If there was a sudden call to arms in the Tractarian War, Ward would call out 'Come along Oakeley' and would rush out of the Common Room. Oakeley would then get up and hop after him." [9]

The new direction is alluded to in Newman's *Apologia.*

"A new school of thought was rising as is usual in doctrinal enquiries and was sweeping the original party of the movement aside and was taking its place...it ate into the movement at an angle and set about turning it."

Wilfred Ward contends that in this new shift Rome was directly looked on as the practical model, the Reformation was a deadly sin, restoration to the Papal Communion an ideal, if unattainable end.

CHAPTER THREE. *The Margaret Chapel Years.*

In 1839 Oakeley was invited to become the minister at the Margaret Chapel near Oxford St in London. Today the site is occupied by All Saints Margaret St, the well known High Anglican Church. Indeed its high church type of service owes much to Oakeley.

The Chapel had already had a varied history when

Oakeley became the missioner. It was opened in 1776 by one David Williams who started off as a dissenting minister at Frome. He later transferred his ministry to Exeter and then to Highgate in London. At this place though he became sceptical as to revealed religion and in 1776 opened the Margaret Chapel for public worship on the principles of Natural Religion apart from Revelation. He published his own "liturgy" for his services from which the name of Christ is altogether absent. The main feature of this Deist worship was a set of antiphons of high flown verbiage recited alternately by minister and people. The number of his supporters fell away and the chapel was closed by 1804. It was then established as a proprietary chapel of the Church of England. In this system the owner of the buildings can nominate his own minister but that minister must obtain a license from the local Bishop to officiate there. Sibthorp officiated at such a chapel in Ryde as will be shown later. The site was obtained by Henry Drummond, a noted Irvingite, but at the time Irvingism was merely a body of beliefs and not a church as such. In 1829 Drummond appointed Charles Dodsworth as his minister.

Dodsworth at the time of his appointment could be classed as an evangelical but during his stay at the Margaret Chapel he moved from that viewpoint through Irvingism to a moderate form of tractarianism.

He attracted quite good congregations it seems, and his friends obtained for him larger premises in Albany St. Oakeley came to know Dodsworth well from around 1836 when he would occasionally assist him. After his removal to Albany St there was a short lived period when the minister was the Rev. Charles Thornton. This gentleman resigned in 1839 and the living was offered to a Fellow of one of the colleges of Oxford who had no spiritual charge at the time and who was known to wish for the opportunity of trying the effect of Tractarian principles on a practical scale.[10]

Oakeley in his memoirs paints an interesting picture both of the area and of the Church at the time he entered upon his ministry:

"[Margaret St] consisted of two parallell lines of moderate sized dwelling houses, most uninterestingly uniform and almost depressingly dismal. Towards its Eastern and more unfashionable end, however, it subsided into a collection of buildings of a more motley character - lodging houses, houses of public entertainment, shops and carriage manufactories. Buried amongst these was a humble structure which the boldest of prophets and the most sanguine of speculators would hardly have ventured to select as the scene of a religious movement and the site of the future Tractarian Cathedral....The Chapel itself was a complete paradigm of ugliness; and all that can be said in its favour is that its architect had adapted it with masterly skill to the uses which it had previously subserved. To the religious and ecclesiastical type it presented a perfect antithesis. It was low dark and stuffy; it bore no other resemblance to the Christian fold than being choked with sheep pens under the name of pews; and its only evidence of being 'surrounded with varieties' was that it was begirt by a hideous gallery, filled on Sundays with uneasy school children. But the triumph of its monstrosities was..in the chancel. From the floor almost to the roof there arose a tripartite structure, beginning with the clerk's desk and terminating in the pulpit, the minister's reading pew occupying the interval. Thus the preacher was elevated on a kind of throne, as if in parody of that which surmounts a Catholic Altar; and there he stood, claiming as it were the adoration of the people....The communion table filled the space behind the reading desk and under the pulpit. The first act of the new minister was to demolish this three headed monster. All attempts at improvement in the general arrangement of the chapel were hopeless and at once abandoned. The congregation which had been somewhat acclimatised to their new position by the efforts of the two preceding ministers bore the change with more equanimity than might have been expected."[11]

The local parish magazine entitled the *Orchestra* related one other important detail. "The desk for the clerk was got rid of; the latter however not without a violent protest from its occupant,...who on the destruction of his place of honour made several futile attempts to erect for himself another in various parts of the chapel. Levelled at last with the congregation he long persisted in uttering the responses in his old style and in the loudest and most discordant tones."

Oakeley too, records that the clerk was a great trial. On one occasion the result was quite amusing. Again let Oakeley describe what happened when Newman was preaching in the Chapel:

> "The clerk occupied rooms adjoining the chapel and communicating by a doorway with its gallery. In these apartments he always seemed to keep a family of cats which had a habit of diffusing themselves over the chapel. To the incumbent for the time being, there was something singularly and perhaps unduly repulsive in the notion of cats in a church. Could it be that the clerk kept these creatures as ministers of his wrath and avengers of his insulted dignity...a train of obsequious furies to be let loose at pleasure?... Sometimes during the First Lesson for instance one of these animals would utter its peculiar cry from some obscure corner or indefinite abyss... on a memorable occasion one of them more adventurous than its companions advanced to the balustrade of the gallery and there perched herself like a fiend. In that instance the clerk did come to the aid of offended discipline and proceeded from his place by stealthy step to arrest the culprit. What was the inevitable consequence? The cat hearing a measured tread behind her, chose with a ready instinct, the only practicable alternative and accordingly by a strong leap descended headlong into the sanctuary, only just clearing the head of an eminent divine (Newman) who happened on that day to be assisting as it were pontifically at morning service!"[12]

But what about the type of service, the liturgy, the music, the style of sermons which were introduced? First of all, little by little the communion table became more and more decorated. Candles appeared, an altar cloth, more elaborate vestments. Bishop Blomfield came to hear of the strange happenings and summoned Oakeley to give an account of his ministry. Indeed in his MS autobiography Oakeley states that he was often summoned to the episcopal presence. He describes such visits rather graphically: "[The waiting room] was like a dentists ante room in which the expectant patients are seated in grim array awaiting their summons to the crucial operation." There was however little that the Bishop could do except request that he make small alterations to the furnishings and did not in fact preach directly Catholic doctrine.

In the end this is exactly what Oakeley did, but to start with Ward told him to stick to moral principles in his sermons until he was well established. He had always had a good name as a preacher. Many were familiar with his oratory from his Whitehall sermons. Now they flocked to Margaret Street. Apart from those who resided nearby, the Church was attended by members of the aristocracy, and more than one person in high official position. Gladstone for instance was a regular visitor and once again in spite of Oakeley's move to Rome, they remained on friendly terms and indeed Gladstone was known to visit Duncan Terrace Islington even when Prime Minister.

So at the Margaret Chapel Oakeley set about introducing Catholic practices and teaching Catholic truths at first with moderation but soon with ever increasing fervour. He was subject to restrictions such as an order that there be only one bouquet of flowers on the communion table, that there could be candles but they could not be lit, that money could be collected on a dish but not in a bag as that was considered a Popish practice. However he was told that he should not gaze intently on the alms dish as people might think it was being worshipped! Finally Oakeley was told he could preach in a surplice in the morning provided he wore a black gown in the evening. All these petty restrictions are described by Oakeley as an attempt to neutralise Rome by Geneva!

One of his chief claims to fame at Margaret Street was the introduction of Plainsong from Solesmes into the worship. Now at last Lloyds lectures were bearing fruit in practice. The specific idea of having plainsong chants followed from a visit to Mount St Bernard's monastery where he witnessed for the first time the full splendour and glory of Catholic ritual and chant. He wrote an article in the

British Critic entitled 'Rites and Ceremonies' This article was in effect a review of Dom Gueranger's *Institutions Liturgiques*. In the article Oakeley called on the Anglican Churches to overcome their nationality and reassert the unity of the undivided Church by the adoption of the eucharist as the chief form of Christian Worship marked by ceremonial actions not found at Morning and Evening Prayer and by the singing of Gregorian Chant.

This was followed up by the publication of a work entitled *The Psalter and Canticles in the Morning and Evening Service of the Church of England set and pointed to Gregorian tones* by R.Redhead with a preface by Frederick Oakeley. Redhead was organist at the Chapel.

Gladstone thought highly of the liturgy at Margaret Chapel and wrote of Oakeley later in the *Contemporary Magazine* "as having united to a firm musical taste, a much finer and rarer gift of discerning and expressing the harmony between the inward purposes of Christian Worship and its outward investiture." [13] After 1841 he followed Dodsworth's model of services at Albany St but with even greater splendour. He took to reciting the breviary hours in a small oratory attended by his friends, who included Gladstone himself together with Robert Williams M.P. and A.J. Beresford Hope who was a great benefactor of the Chapel.

By 1845 Benjamin Webb was able to write to J.M. Neale, (well known even today as a hymn writer) "They have got up a complete musical Mass, commandments, Epistle, Gospel, Preface, all sung to ancient music." However at the very end of his life Oakeley made it clear that he never claimed to say Mass at the Margaret Chapel.

> "I can honestly say that the motive which actuated me in trying to improve upon the ceremonial practice..was to give worship as much reverential beauty as was consistent with the strict observance of such rubrics as were plain and incontrovertible, and the free interpretation of others which seemed to me to admit without undue straining of a more catholic sense than that which they commonly received...I

must maintain that the ritual at Margaret Chapel, whatever may be said for or against it, was simplicity itself...no Catholic however uneducated, could possible have mistaken the Communion Service at Margaret Chapel for High Mass."

(Quoted from *Good and Faithful Servants* by Peter Galloway and Christopher Rawll, Worthing, 1988")

What about the sermons he preached at this time? A large number of his sermons were printed at the time. On the 10th November 1844 he preached about outward observances and the spirit in which they are peformed.

"Now we must certainly call it 'straining at a gnat and swallowing a camel' where...the same persons who would be quite uneasy at the mere circumstance of missing church, have no scruple about for example wearing finery above their station or being harsh to the poor, or entertaining ill will against their neighbours, or in other ways, violating justice mercy and faith, while they are even punctilious about an action which has no merit whatever in God's sight but that it is the fruit of the Spirit."

Later in the same sermon he writes:

"Of course if there be any one mere act which is precious on its own account, Holy Communion is that one. And yet my brethren, you will many of you, I am sure, bear me out in saying that even this most solemn and blessed of all actions MAY be performed too much as a matter of custom and routine, so that the mere casual ommission of of it might come to seem a greater sin than the irreverent participation of it, or than the wilful and even habitual neglect of some great duty of the Christian life." [14]

In the following week he returned to the same point. He argues that if we overvalue small details there is a tendency to come into a state of anxiety about them. He writes:

"[There may be]..disquietude of soul at the mere circumstance of ommitting them even casually, so as to seriously prejudice Christian confidence and peace of mind..this particular sort of overscrupulousness, a person is in no danger of till he becomes conscientious; and indeed the one great reason among others why the evil in question has been hardly even so much as heard of among us till quite of late is this, that conscientiousness itself has been too little recognised as an essential part of the Christian character. But now through the dissemination of books of a higher tone of religion, we are beginning to understand something not merely of the nature of sanctity as distinct from ordinary virtue, but of its peculiar trials and temptations also.." [15]

After the publication of Tract 90 which is in essence at attempt to understand the 39 articles of the protestant faith in a Catholic sense, Oakeley became more and more Roman. He wrote a noteworthy article in the magazine *British Critic* in which he tries to show that the English version of the Reformation was not as protestant in ethos as on the continent, while on the other hand it was by no means of course entirely Catholic. What caused most offense to those who were not tractarians was the implication that the Church of England had to go forward in a Catholic direction.

"The object important as it may be in itself, is quite inadequate to the sacrifice. We cannot stand where we are; we must go backwards or forwards; and it will surely be the latter....And as we go on we must recede more and more from the principles, if there be any, of the English Reformation."

In the article also he denounces the so called liberty of conscience and inalienable right of private judgement when applied to matters doctrinal. When attacked on this point he wrote an open letter to one of his critics, Rev. Charles Smith Bird, late fellow of Trinity Cambridge.

"Let us consider Protestantism in the point of view in which you take pleasure in exhibiting it; as a religion based on the exercise of private judgement...Is it not obvious that we must all be agreed upon the truth to which men are to be converted before we can attempt to convert them? Yet your rules make union and unity impossible."

By the start of 1845 Oakeley's position as minister was becoming impossible. The axe was about to fall.

CHAPTER FOUR.

The End at Margaret Street. Oakeley's Conversion.

The events which led to the conversion of most of the Oxford Movement men were now close at hand. The publication of Tract 90 was as it were the beginning of the end. Towards the end of 1844 W.G. Ward published his famous work. *The Ideal of a Christian Church considered in comparision with Existing Practice.* In effect Ward tried to show that the Roman Catholic Church was the all but perfect embodiment of the Christian idea and ethos.

It was clear that Ward would be censored and Oakeley wrote an "open letter" to the Vice Chancellor of Oxford in defence of Ward.

He asked for the support of all those who still had an open mind amongst the members of convocation who would try Ward. He also wrote to the Bishop of London defending his actions in this matter.

Ward was degraded at a special meeting of convocation on the 13th February 1845. Bishop Blomfield was now determined to rid himself of Oakeley. Sergeant Bellasis wrote to Oakeley:

> "We hear from some friends in this quarter that you and your chapel are under consideration by the Bishop and that he says openly at his dinner table that he will either have your book of Devotions for Holy Communion or the Chapel removed."

Writing to Mr Blandy on Feb 28th Bellasis says

> "We have had a very hard fight...Oakeley made up his mind that if he was to go it must be at the Bishop's own responsibility and his friends in London beset the Bishop (Blomfield) on all sides. Gladstone wrote to him, Williams and I called on him but all to no purpose; the only thing that frightened him was that Coleridge told him plainly that although he did not agree with Oakeley, yet that an interference even with an extreme person on the one side, without interfering with extreme persons on the other, was a position he could not support....This shook the Bishop and he

took the opinion of Dr.Lushington whether Oakeley's letter to the Vice Chancellor was inconsistent with his subscription (to the 39 articles) and he replied that it was a very difficult question...so doubtful that he advised him not to act against Oakeley." [16]

The reprieve was only short lived. Following the degradation of Ward, Oakeley published another "open letter" to his friends in the Church of England. The letter is dated 19th February but it was not published until 25th June. The letter is a defence of his position at Margaret Street. He writes:

> "I said to myself that I will not so much as entertain the thought of leaving the Ministry still less the Communion of the Church of England as long as I can fulfill the conditions she imposes upon me with a safe conscience. I am deliberately and as I believe finally, satisfied that there is no standing ground between Protestantism and the Roman theology. It is Rome alone which seems to me to propose doctrines on the authority of the Church. As soon as I leave this firm basis I get adrift and am thrown in one way or another upon private judgement, private views of Scripture, or of Antiquity, or of both. If Our Lord has left a Church on earth, that Church must be *toties quoties* the authorised expositress of His Word and I see no Church but the Roman which even claims to fulfill this office for the Christian World. On the other hand, Almighty God of his good purpose has placed me in the Church of England; there I will by his help abide while I may; I have a work to do where I am; I will not be the person to cut the knot...."

Oakeley was as the title of his letter indicates claiming to HOLD as distinct from TEACH the doctrines of the Catholic Churchletter.He ends his letter:

> "If you recognise the Church of England as a branch of the Catholic Church, we consider that the manifestation of earnest Catholic sympathies at any rate gives us a claim on your indulgence..If you will not let us hold what we forbear to teach you may drive us where we may teach as well as

hold; it is a question for you and not for us." [17]

The Bishop was now bound to act firmly. He instigated a suit against Oakeley at the Court of Arches for the suspension of his license on the grounds that he was not teaching the 39 articles but rather Catholic doctrine. Oakeley offered to resign but the Bishop refused to accept the resignation being determined that the matter should be aired in court.

The Court of Arches is the Provincial Court of Canterbury. At the time of Oakeley's trial the Dean of Arches was a certain Sir Herbert Jenner Fust. The advocates in the court were required to hold doctorates in civil law from Oxford or Cambridge before being allowed to practice at the Court of Arches. Fust himself was also the judge at the famous Gorham Judgement which led to Manning's departure from the Church of England. Oakeley decided first to resign his license on the 3rd July 1845 and the trial began at once.

Weary of the strife, Oakeley refused to defend himself. Bellasis relates that he told the court "Work your will gentleman, but I will neither seek your aid, nor deprecate your conclusions." Oakely then refused to defend himself and the trial became more or less a debate between the prosecution counsel and the Judge. Judgement was therefore against Oakeley by default but Justice Fust would not let the matter rest there. He issued a long judgement in which he shows clearly that it is impossible to accept the 39 articles in a Catholic Sense. The Articles and Catholic doctrine are simply not compatible.

The judgement is worth quoting for it is surely just as relevant today as it was when it was written.

> "By the 39 articles alone would the court test the soundness of Mr Oakeley's opinions...It had been truly stated in argument that these articles had been drawn up in direct opposition to the doctrines laid down in the council of Trent. Mr Oakeley had assumed as true the doctrines of that council and those doctrines seemed only to be a repetition

of the former doctrines of the Church of Rome. What then - to pass over the first five - WAS the sixth article of the Church of England? 'That Holy Scripture contained everything necessary to salvation, and that anything not written therein nor proved thereby was not required to be believed by any man.'

The foundation of the Church of England then was that here doctrines rested exclusively upon Scripture but the Church of Rome in addition to the Scriptures added Tradition and placed Tradition upon the same footing as, and made it of equal authority with, Scripture.

This was an obvious distinction and formed an insuperable barrier to the union of the two churches. The 19th and 21st articles of the church of England were pretty much to the same effect. In them was a positive re-affirmation of the doctrine laid down in the sixth article. Upon that article what possible doubt or cavil could be raised ? By what mental reservation could Mr Oakeley have avoided the plain and obvious meaning of this doctrine? On the other hand under the pain of anathema the Church of Rome required tradition to be received as the same binding authority as scripture. The court asked then by what means could any man 'extort', let alone 'extract', any Catholic or Roman meaning from the sixth article of the Church?

The court would pass over the doctrines of original sin, the works of supererogation and other doctrines, not because there was no distinction between the opinion of the two churches on these points but because the distinction between them would be more easily traced in some others. The court would pause at the 23rd article which pronounced purgatory and the invocation of the saints as "not to be proved by scripture but as rather repugnant thereto". By what mental reservation could this article again be received in a Catholic sense? The article itself stated that these doctrines were the doctrines of the Roman church, the whole range of which Oakeley believed. He therefore, differing from his church, believed that purgatory was ' no vain thing'. The doctrine of purgatory had been known long before the Council of Trent, but it was not necessary to refer to the Church of Rome. The court must assume that the doctrine of purgatory was a Romish doctrine. From the article of the Church of England it was so stated to be. The article repudiated and renounced that doctrine but from his own admission, Mr Oakeley must clearly support and maintain it. The court would next refer to the fifth article in which all the sacraments except the two of Baptism and the Lord's supper, were rejected as not being of Divine authority. What then was the doctrine of Rome on the question of the Sacraments? It was to be found in the 7th section of the Council of Trent. There instead of two sacraments, seven sacraments were appointed and of those seven, several, specially and by name rejected in the articles of the Church of England were receieved and decreed by the Church of Rome under the pain of anathema.....The Court would next refer to the doctrine with regard to the Supper of the Lord. Transubstantiation was in the article clearly rejected, but in the section of the Council of Trent anno 1551, that doctrine was positively laid down. Here again was a positive contradiction and irreconcilable difference. The canons of the Church of Rome were, too, as strong in favour of transubstantiation as the decrees of the council of Trent. That doctrine had been laid down in the councils of Lateran and Constance.

The carrying about of the Eucharistic elements was equally the subject of differences between the Churches. How was Mr Oakeley to get out of these difficulties ?

In the mind of the court it was impossible to raise a doubt as to the sense or meaning of the words used in the article. The receiving of the sacrament in both kinds, was no less a matter of difference between the Church of England and the Church of Rome. In the 21st section of the Countil of Trent (anno 1562), it was laid down that one kind alone should be administered to the laity, and by the articles of the Church of England this doctrine was as distinctly denied. The sacrifice of the Mass was by the Church of England declared to be blasphemous and vain, but the Church of Rome under the pain of anathema decreed the observance of that service as a propitaitary sacrifice. Was it necessary for the court to go further than this?" [18]

The judgement was given on June 30th and the result clear. Oakeley was to be permanently suspended from all ministry until such time as he retracted the views he held to the satisfaction of his Bishop.

So Oakeley had to pack his bags and depart. At that moment he had no clear idea of what would happen. He first spent a few weeks with Ward in the country and then moved to Oxford. He spent some time at Littlemore with Newman and his companions and was there when Fr. Dominic came to receive the future Cardinal into the Church. That date was the 9th October 1845 and Oakeley himself was received by Fr Newsham SJ at St Clement's Chapel in Oxford. A few days later he was confirmed with Newman and his companions at Oscott by Bishop Wiseman.

In a letter to a friend, later published, Oakeley wrote

> "I bow myself before her because she plainly corresponds with that type of Catholic Church which is deeply and habitually impressed upoon my whole moral and spiritual nature in those very particulars in which the Anglican Church has for some time been failing and has at length ceased to correspond with it....Apostasy, secession, desertion; these and the like are the terms by which such acts (conversions) are habitually denoted. This I think shows how little people realise even the theory of a divided Church. They speak more like members of a club than of one section of the Church Catholic."

He remained at Littlemore only a short while and seems to have taken temporary lodgings in Oxford during November. At the start of December Newman reported to his friends that Oakeley had decided to study for the priesthood at St. Edmund's College Ware. Most of the converts seemed to have preferred Oscott but in Oakeley's case the reason for the choice was his existing friendship with the vice Rector Dr Whitty. A few years earlier Oakeley had written an article on auricular confession which impressed Whitty and they met up to discuss the points raised at that time. Another factor in favour of Ware was that Ward had decided to live there. As he had married he could not now become a priest but by arrangement he had a house designed and built by Pugin and situated in the grounds of the College.

Oakeley entered St Edmund's on 22nd January 1846 and was ordained at the college by Bishop Wiseman on the 14th November 1847. He was then appointed assistant at St.George's Cathedral, Southwark.

Chapter Five
Oakeley's Life as a Catholic Priest and a Canon of Westminster

Oakeley must have been very relieved to become a Catholic Priest at last. His year at St. Edmund's had been spoilt by some very undignified controversy. A novel entitled *From Oxford to Rome and Back* was published in April by an anonymous author. It later transpired that the author was a certain Miss E.F. Harris, whom Oakeley had been advising about becoming a Catholic. The book contained a slanderous attack on the converts and in particular one who could be clearly identified as Oakeley. As early as June the attacks on him personally started up. *The Tablet* (June 19th 1847) reported that the influential *Church and State Gazette* had published an article calling Oakeley a hypocrite in that as an Anglican he had received orders too quickly without the customary year's interval between diaconate and priesthood, and that the speed with which he received orders was due to his desire to become a fellow of Balliol.

The article had then found its way into the columns of *The Times.*

Luckily for Oakeley a refutation of this attack was published in *The Tablet* by "Fellow of Balioll", (almost certainly Ward). The writer pointed out that although the priesthood was usually delayed by a year after the diaconate, the Anglican Bishops had the right to dispense from this rule if the candidate was of outstanding quality. Also that Oakeley had been preparing for the life of a cleric for some time.

In August *The Tablet* published a recantation by the unknown author of *From Oxford to Rome*, and coupled this with a letter of acceptance from Oakeley. He writes "The expectation of aid and comfort in the Catholic Church which he expressed before his conversion has been subsequently realised." Yet two weeks later the author felt obliged to publish a 2nd recantation. It seems that her brother and a certain Rev.W.F. Lloyd had been putting it about that the recantation had been actually been forced on her by Oakeley.

This information was again carried by *The Church and State Gazette*. Finally in the issue for September 11th, full details of all the correspondence were published. From this, one can see that Oakeley had been accused of abusing the (Anglican) Confessional, and being in favour of the compulsory separation of wives from husbands in the event of only one party being converted to the Catholic Church. This of course in addition to the general charge of hypocrisy over Oakeley's conversion and his supposed desire to return to the Anglican Fold. This time the author reveals herself as Miss E.F. Harris and Oakeley writes a final letter to clear up his involvement.

In Rome, Newman on hearing of his friend's difficulties wrote the novel *Loss and Gain* in order to clarify for the general public the true nature of conversion. Oakeley was eternally grateful, for as late as 1855 he printed the text of a lecture he gave at Islington entitled

"Personal Reminiscences of the Oxford Movement with Illustrations from Dr. Newman's *Loss and Gain*". About half his long talk is given over to direct quotations from "*Loss and Gain*".

After his ordination Oakeley was sent to St. George's Southwark.

When he went there the Cathedral was nearing

completion but Mass was still being said in the London Road Chapel. His immediate superior was the redoutable Dr. Doyle who had done so much to ensure that St. George's was built. He was however a rather eccentric character who seems to have spent most of his spare time in writing verbose letters to the "Tablet" and other journals on any matter that took his fancy.

His fellow assistants included Fr. James Danell who later became the 2nd Bishop of Southwark, Fr. John Wheble who would later die out in the Crimea as a Chaplain, and the notorious Fr. (later Monsignor) George Talbot who would quickly be posted to Rome to become an agent for the Bishops. He became a confidant of Manning during the difficulties between Manning and the rest of the Westminster Chapter.

Oakeley would have been present when Newman and his new Oratorians including Coffin, came to preach a Lenten Mission at St.George's which turned out to be a resounding disaster. Then came the great day of the opening of the Cathedral, the 4th July 1848. Fourteen Bishops attended and about 300 clergy. The 'Times' reported that the procession which took over 15 minutes to enter the building was quite impressive but when it came to the clergy the correspondent reported " This part of the procession was quite remarkable for the number of ugly faces it contained, an ugliness which under the circumstances could hardly be considered as either picturesque or imposing." Furthermore Doyle's management skills were clearly lacking for after they entered it was discovered that no particular Bishop had been invited to say the Mass.

Bishop Wiseman had only been asked to preach , so in the event he had to sing the Mass as well.

During the week following the opening a special octave of services was held with special preachers each day including the oratorians Dalgairns and Faber and Oakeley himself on the 3rd day. On the octave day also his oratorical powers were required at a Pontifical High Mass celebrated by the Bishop of Liege. Once the Cathedral was opened Doyle was particularly fond of laying on grand ceremonies. The choir too had to be of the best. A rather amusing incident relating to the choir involved Oakeley. Shortly after he had left for Islington a report appeared that the choir included ladies. Oakeley responded by writing

> "I believe I am correct in saying that the Bishop of that diocese shares the objection which the Cardinal Archbishop also feels to female voices of any description in Ecclesiastical choirs..the mistake has probably arisen from the choir of St.George's occasionally having been strengthened by other instruments than the organ, a practice to which our superiors do not object." Dr Doyle's management was also called into question by Oakeley in a letter to the Bishop dated 31st July 1849. During Exposition of the Blessed Sacrament on a Sunday afternoon, a young girl was ejected by the doorman who told her the church was always closed between Mass and Vespers. The mother had complained to Oakeley who discovered there had been a "misunderstanding" between Doyle and the doorman. He claimed he did not know the girl and she was kept out under the plea of "protection against the innocent".

There is certainly a hint of snobbery here. The congregation was quite mixed. As a Cathedral the services attracted a large number of wealthy patrons who came to enjoy the music while the basic congregation was very poor indeed.

His stay at Southwark lasted less than two years. Towards the end of 1849 Bishop Wiseman informed him that he was to take over the parish of St. John the Evangelist, Duncan Terrace, Islington. Oakeley was overjoyed. According to the Manuscript at Balliol this was precisely the Parish he had always wanted! When it was built in 1843 it was the largest Catholic Church in London. The author of the "Catholic Handbook" of 1845 writes of it.

> "Entering by the large doors in the street facade we have before us an uninterrupted sweep of one hundred and

> thirty seven feet, six inches. The height to the ridge is about seventy feet and the clear width between the main walls forty feet. The range of windows in the clerestory is in perfect keeping with the whole structure - bold high raised, uniform and very impressive." Later he tells us that "There are a number of paintings in this church, five of which copied by himself from celebrated masterpieces have been presented by Mr Kenelm Digby."

Oakeley entered his new Parish on the 26th January 1850 and remained there until he died on 29th January 1880. The start up was hardly auspicious. The previous Rector was still in the house and refused to go. It took about one month to persuade him to leave. Furthermore he found to his horror that the choir was composed of the dreaded females, but as he explains in the Balliol Manuscript, he soon changed all that and introduced a choir of men and boys! Indeed like Margaret Street, Islington would under Oakeley become well known for the glory of its ceremonies and music.

The area was quite mixed. Down the road lived the original model for the character of the 'Artful Dodger' in 'Oliver Twist', while at the other end of the spectrum one could find at least for a couple of years, Caroline Chisholm who would later do such great work in Australia. It is believed that Caroline persuaded Oakeley to compose the hymn to St. Andrew which is still to be found in Hymn books particularly those used in Scotland. Another resident in the early days was Julian Tenison-Woods. The Tenison-Woods family were distantly related by marriage to the Oakeley family. In 1843 Julian had been taken on as a pupil by Oakeley while he was at Margaret Street. In 1848 he was instructed by Oakeley and received into the Catholic Church. He moved to Islington with Oakeley and stayed for about two years until he joined the Passionist Order. In later life he emigrated to Australia where he founded two religious orders and somehow managed to combine a very busy life as a missioner with lecturing on scientific and geological topics to learned societies in that vast continent. He published his final scientific work on *The anatomy of the Life History of Mollusca peculiar to Australia* in 1888.[19]

Returning now to Islington, a flavour of the devotional life of the Parish can be gleaned from the pages of the 'Catholic Directory' in any year during the 1850's or 1860's. The entry hardly varies. The assistant priests are given as William Ignatius Dolan and Andrew Mooney. They remained with their Parish Priest nearly all the time he was there. Dolan was an accomplished organist and helped with the choir. The Sunday Masses were at 7,8,9, 10, and 11.00 am High Mass. Catechism at 3.00pm, Vespers and Benediction at 7.00pm. Benediction also took place every Thursday plus feasts of Our Lord and Our Lady. Rosary or devotions took place every other day at 8.00pm unless the Sacred Heart devotions were being recited on certain Fridays or the Confraternity devotions on certain Wednesdays. Two confraternities were listed, the Blessed Sacrament, and the Immaculate Heart of Mary. Devotions to Our Lady took place daily in May and during November for the Holy Souls.

During 1850 the Catholic Hierarchy was re-established in England and Wales with Wiseman as Archbishop of Westminster and a Cardinal. Islington with London north of the Thames now became part of the new Diocese of Westminster instead of being part of London District.

Oakeley was appointed a Chapter Canon in 1852, the year of the commencement of Chapters in all dioceses. Now it is quite well known that the Westminster Chapter came to have serious differences with Cardinal Wiseman over certain aspects of administration and later over the question of the Westminster Succession. These differences together with the differences with Bishop Grant of Southwark in which the Westminster Chapter again sided with their cousins across the Thames, are well documented in the standard histories of the time and it would be pointless to go over the same ground again here. The differences were most acute from about 1856 until

Wiseman's death.

Only Manning who quickly joined the Chapter after his ordination supported Wiseman . This was inevitable as one of the problems concerned the influence of the Oblates of St Charles were having at St. Edmund's Ware. Manning had started up the Oblates himself.

Certainly in the 5 years before his accession, relations between Manning and Oakeley were distinctly cool. For instance in a letter to Talbot in Rome Manning writes that the Westminster Canons, O'Neal, Maguire Oakeley and Weathers are not fit to have even a voice in the choice of any Archbishop of Westminster. Again in 1864 after the publication of Newman's Apologia he writes to Talbot that "Maguire and Oakeley are making fools of themselves." This refers to their efforts to publicise the 'Apologia' which had given great offence to Manning as the great man was not even mentioned in the book !

A little light on relations between Oakeley and Manning is shed by a couple of letters from Oakeley to George Talbot in Rome (now preserved in the archives of the English College). In these we learn that Oakeley tried to keep clear of active intervention in the controversies but like all the other chapter members he objected very much to the position of Manning as their provost when they all considered that his position as head of the Oblates was not really compatible with being head of the Chapter. Oakeley also wrote strongly about the Oblates in general. He considered them as not really suited for the kind of work they had to do in the Westminster Diocese. His letters are however written as between friends. Little did he know that such information would quickly be passed back to Manning who was about the only person in England that Talbot supported ! When the chapter put forward the name of Bishop Errington to succeed Wiseman we find Oakeley writing to Talbot again attempting to excuse the choice of the canons. He pointed out that when they made the choice they were not aware of how much pain that would cause the Holy Father. Also that the final voting at the chapter in favour of Errington as the chosen candidate was only 6 votes in favour to 5 against. The implication of the leter is that Oakeley did not in fact support Errington at the vote.

However after Manning's succession all was peace and light again.

Weathers became an auxiliary Bishop and the only time when even the slightest problem between Manning and Oakeley arose was an incident in 1874 when Oakeley had been invited to one of Gladstone's 'Thursday Breafasts'. When Oakeley informed Manning of the invitation he replied that he would take it as a personal affront if any of his priests should visit Gladstone's house. It is not clear whether Oakeley actually attended the breakfast but he certainly met up with Gladstone and informed him of Manning's remark for he related later tht Gladstone became visibly affected and there was 'almost a vindictive gleam in his eye'. Oakeley recorded that he thought the action of the Cardinal was bad policy, not in keeping with his wonted diplomacy, to leave Gladstone to the exclusive influence of Lord Acton. It should be noted that it was about this time that Gladstone had launched an attack on the recently defined doctrine of Papal Infallibility and this had severed relations altogether between Manning and Gladstone.

Manning's attitude towards Oakeley after he became Archbishop is better shown in the episode in which Manning tried hard for a reconciliation with Newman. This took place during the latter half of 1867. The initiative came from Manning. The entire correspondence can be found in Purcell's *Life of Cardinal Manning* Vol Two, pages 327 to 346. Manning chose Oakeley as an intermediary between himself and Newman. Such was the suspicion between Manning and Newman that some of the letters were sent to Oakeley first to be transmitted onwards.

The actual difficulties between them are of no concern here but Oakeley's role as mediator can be noted in these extracts.

Oakeley wrote to Newman on 6 July 1867:

"The Archbishop has more than once expressed to me his great regret that there should exist between himself and you what he feels to be a state of personal alienation and his earnest desire of doing everything in his power to remove it...."

Later on August 14th Manning writes to Oakeley:

" Many thanks for sending me your correspondence with Newman.Whatever comes of it you will have the reward of the peacemakers"

Nothing did in practice come of the correspondence which ceased on 3rd November 1867 when Newman wrote to Manning

"I can only repeat what I said when you last heard from me. I do not know whether I am on my head or my heels when I have active relations with you."

What then of Oakeley's true relationship with Cardinal Wiseman and other Bishops.? Until the Chapter difficulties arose Oakeley was a staunch defender of His Eminence. For instance in 1854 when rumours about Wiseman's poor administration were coming to the fore, largely through the *Rambler*, Oakeley was in Rome and was able to contradict the reports that the rumours had come from certain Oratorians. W.G.Ward was able to write to Wiseman that Oakeley had been able in Rome to counteract certain unfavourable rumours about Wiseman's policy especially that the originators were not Oratorians. Oakeley had indeed been able to give Ward the names of those responsible. Ward however did not name names in his letter to Wiseman.

Even in the midst of the Chapter difficulties Oakeley writes in a kindly style to his Ordinary, and no mention of any problems.

On the 21st Sept 1863 he writes:

"My Dear Lord Cardinal,

I have two objects in writing, the one to ask how you are and the other to congratulate you upon the public response to your lecture at Southampton which I read with since pleasure in the *Times*....We seem to be making great way here. The Church is thronged and the local newspapers are writing us up. Last night after a service in honour of the Seven Dolours, (a humble imitation of the Good Friday meditations with music) a Protestant Gentleman came up to one of the priests and said 'Sir I am not of your religion but such an evening as this is almost enough to make a case for me."

On the 17th October 1864 he asks if His Eminence would come to pontificate at High Mass on the 6th November when "we are going to perform a beautiful Mass of Gounod, the great French Composer, which I should like your Eminence to hear. It is in quite a new style, not long, and very full of melody. Pray come my dear Lord if you can." [18] With reference to other Bishops there is a rather interesting letter to Bishop Grant of Southwark dated 18t April 1861 about prisoners. Oakeley's parish covered Pentonville Prison and Grant had dealings with the government over the access of Catholic Priests to the inmates of prisons. One of the problems of the time was that the prison inspectorate would not let Catholic Priests visit any prisoners other than those on the Governor's List of prisoners who had specially asked for the ministrations of a Priest. Oakeley writes that he had discovered that any Catholic prisoner who attended even in error, a Protestant service is automatically struck off the List of Catholics entitled to see a Priest. He writes too that prisoners are subjected to every possible inducement to attend such services.

Oakeley then asks the Bishop if he can raise the matter on the appropriate committee.

Very early on in his priesthood Oakeley clashed with Bishop Ullathorne who at the time of the Oxford movement had a distinct suspicion of the converts. When in December 1848 the *Rambler* published an article which complained about the poor education that Catholics received, Ullathorne wrote a very intemperate letter about converts.understanding that the *Rambler* Article had been written by a Convert. He wrote in the *Tablet*.

"We have seen a day when those who are but children amongst us, forgetting their pupillage, have undertaken to rebuke, censure and condemn the acts of those in authority in our Church and the sentiments of her members" Oakeley wrote to Wiseman directly in reply;

"I regret the letter especially on its effect on expected conversions from the Anglican Body for I know of an opinion widely prevailing that the more excellent of the most recent converts, the more learned devoted self denying zealous, are not appreciated among us."

CHAPTER SIX
Final Years. Oakeley's Writings as a Catholic.

The treatment of Oakeley's years as a Catholic Priest has been somewhat sketchy. The fact is that we know far more about him as an Anglican than a Catholic. He did not leave any autbiographical writings on the last 30 years of his life which were spent relatively quietly as a Parish Priest. One might well wonder why he did not progress any further into the English Hierarchy. There could be several reasons for this. In general the Oxford Converts were the wrong age to become Bishops when the chance arose, (excepting Manning of course). They were not eligible when the English Hierarchy was restored in 1850 as they had barely been ordained at that time. The episcopacy was as it were "open" to them only after say 1860 when the first generation of the new Hierarchy started dying off. By then many were already elderly or in poor health. Oakeley is a case in point.

He was always lame and after 1864 he lost the sight of one eye and very slowly started losing sight of the other eye, though never entirely blind. Tom Mozley paints a rather sad picture of him in his final years.

"Nobody cared less for himself or took less care of himself. He might be seen limping about the streets of London...a mis-shapen fabric of bare bones upon which hung some very shabby canonicals. Yet his eye was bright and his voice though sorrowful was kind,and he was always glad to greet an old friend..There was always something aristocratic even in the wreck.." [21]

Gladstone backs up this picture in a letter to R.W. Church in 1880 when Church was gathering material for his own book on the movement.

"Poor Oakeley, I have always thought of him as one of the converts of 44 or 45 who had sacrificed much that the natural man cares for. He was a man whose quality and whose craving was refinement,not strength or exactness or ascertained truth or originality of any kind, but the grace and beauty of finish. He was just the man to pass a happy and useful life writing elegant and interesting lectures and sermons and enjoying music and art and good talk without luxury or selfishness as a distinguished Anglican Clergyman. The Romans made nothing of him but sent him up to Islington to live poorly in a poor house with two Irish colleagues with just a print or two and a few books remaining of the Oxford wreck which was the overthrow of his old idea of life. And he was to the last as far as I saw him, interested in nothing so much as in the gossip of the old days and he was always kindly, patient, and gentle not without touches of amusement when talking of people who did not think with him. It was like a genuine bit of the old Balliol Common Room set in the frame of this dingy Islington parlour." [22]

Only a few years earlier though Gladstone had written in the *Contemporary Review* for October, 1874

"The papal Church now enjoys the advantages of the labours of Mr Oakeley who united to a fine musical taste a much finer and much rarer gift in discerning and expressing the harmony between the inward purposes of Christian worship and its outward investiture".

Oakeley died on January 29th 1880 and was buried at Kensal Green cemetery on the 5th of February. The funeral Mass was conducted by Bishop Weathers, auxiliary in Westminster in the presence of Cardinal Manning who preached the panegyric.

The Cardinal told the congregation that Oakeley had especially requested that the Cardinal should say a few words at his funeral. He pointed out that he had known Oakeley as a friend since 1827 and that only "His venerable brother in the Sacred College" (ie. Newman) had known him longer, his memory stretching back to 1820. He continued

> "The time had been full of events and among them was one in which both Frederick Oakeley and himself had a share; in the pouring down of the Holy Ghost and in that sensible inspiration which has passed over England. These were events not from men, nor of men, but from the Holy Ghost. No human influence, no human intellect, no human power wrought these changes. He had watched over Frederick Oakeley from that hour to this day and he might say that they had hardly ever been parted. His venerable brother (Newman) of whom he had spoken, watched over him also but at a distance; but he watched over him close at hand. He had been his fellow labourer and for more than 25 years they were closely united; but during the last fifteen years they had been bound together by a far closer tie, a far more intimate confidence, and therefore if anyone could speak of Frederick Oakeley, he could. He was a true disciple of Jesus Christ in the fullness of the word, loving, holy, harmless, self-denying, laborious in his masters service...He was a true priest, penetrated by the sacerdotal unction from head to foot.He was a true pastor labouring for souls. He was a kind and loving friend. None that ever appraoched him could forget his loving, kindly, gentle, cheerful, playful sweet tone of voice, and aspect and countenance, and the maturity of his thought, and the wisdom of his words..."[23]

Oakeley was a prolific writer but almost everything he wrote has been totally forgotten except for one item. He is the translator of that most popular Carol "Adeste Fideles" into English as "O Come all ye faithful." Perhaps it is unfortunate to start with this, as the translation contains that dreadful line "Lo, he abhors not the virgin's womb." The carol itself is of interest. Composed by John Wade in 1742 for use as a hymn to be sung after Vespers of

Christmas at Douai College where students for the priesthood were trained in the days of persecution, it is said to be a coded message of the impending arrival in England of Prince Charles Edward Stuart. "Regem Angelorum" could be understood as "Regem Anglorum" and Bethlehem understood as England.

It is a known fact that Wade wrote coded hymns but we will never be certain about "O come all ye faithful"

Oakeley also wrote "Praise we Our God with Joy" in collaboration with others and the hymn to St.Andrew. Other hymns in his book *Lyra Liturgica* are now forgotten. Sometimes he went right "over the top"in sentimentality. For instance here are two verses from the "Centenary Ode" composed for the Centenary of Old Hall College Ware in 1869:

Awake my lyre Awake!
A theme Invites your aid today
No Maudlin poet's idle dream No soft voluptuous lay
Choose ye your parts
Ye filial hearts
That own a nursing Mother's gentle sway.

(In the following verse Mabella was the mother of St.Edmund.)

And many a mother breathed a prayer
in good Mabella's name
That son of hers might win a share
In Edmund's saintly fame

And well I ween,
Our virgin Queen
Did speed in wings of love
that mothers claim.

Perhaps it is just as well he did not limit himself to writing verse. In 1871 he published *The Priest on the Mission* based on a series of sermons given at St. Edmund's Ware in 1869, the same year that is that the above ode was written. The lectures are completely down to earth, filled with practical adivice to young priests making points which are just as valid today as when he first wrote them. So in Chapter Two he deals with different modes of preaching. Having rejected the idea of preaching extempore out of hand, he also finds fault with both reading a sermon from a prepared script or learning it off by heart. The best way is "that of carefully preparing sermons in skeleton as we may say, beforehand, and trusting to our natural powers of expression, improved by habits of training for filling them out in delivery." Later he writes

> "With regard to the more difficult task of putting these materials into effective shape at the time of delivery, the first piece of advice I would venture to give you is that if you adopt this plan of writing out the whole or any considerable part of your sermon, you should be very careful to FORGET putting your manuscript into your pocket. I am not speaking of mere notes which may be useful to you in suggesting the order of topics, but of any such part of your composition as might supply you with the very words to be used. If while you are preaching, you feel that this paper is at your command, you will be apt to hanker and fidget after it instead of trying to do your best in expressing the sense, not in reproducing the words, of what you have written."

Other chapters in this book deal with visiting the sick and prisoners, working with young people and care of the Church.

In 1857 Oakeley published another set of sermons, this time somewhat adapted, that he had preached at Islington. These sermons were particularly directed to non-Catholics of whom a large number were it seems in the habit of coming to listen to Oakeley. These sermons seek to show that the truths of the Catholic faith are quite compatible with the words of Holy Scripture and to answer various charges made against the faith. The book is entitled *The Church of the Bible*. Here is what he has to say about laxity in religion based on supposed practice in the confessional. (page 211)

> "The Catholic is said to be a lax religion, which holds out the right hand of fellowship to indifferent sort of people. You will often see persons of very suspicious character crowding around our confessionals; and when they come out they show, by their very gait and manner, that they have received some extraordinary encouragement. This comes, you are inclined to suspect, of a lax system of morality, which pampers the profligate at the expense of the repectable. Moreover you are apt to observe, that it is the 'black sheep' of the family who becomes a Catholic. It is often the spendthrift or the outcast rather than the more orderly and well conducted inmates of their father's household, who turn up when we least expect it, in the Catholic Church. Often indeed, it is otherwise; yet the connection between a youth of sin and an age of Catholic devotion is certainly common enough to justify the impression that there is some point of contact between the two states. Now is it not very curious that our Blessed Saviour was subjected to precisely the same charge which the Catholic Church now has to endure? Turn to St. Luke Chapter 15 and you will find there that your Divine Redeemer vindicates Himself from the imputation of receiving sinners and eating with them, not by denying the fact but by explaining the reason of such condescension."

One of the most eclectic or perhaps eccentric books with which Oakeley was connected is entitled *The Catholic Florist - A Guide to the Cultivation of Flowers for the Altar...and fragments of Ecclesiastical Poetry*. This came out in 1850. The only section entirely by Oakeley is the preface. He points out how many flowers have had their names changed from religious titles like "the snowdrop whose pure white flowers are the first harbingers of Spring and is noted down in some calendars as an emblem of the Purification of the Spotless Virgin Mother. It blooms about Candlemas and was formerly known by the more religious designation of "Fair maids of February".

He also reminded readers about the attitude of the

Bishop of London when he was at Margaret Street.

"As a method of Church decorations it has fallen under the ban of Church condemnation in the Establishment and not many years ago the writer of these lines was himself inhibited when an Anglican Minister, from attempting to interest his congregation through the medium of 'Flowers on the Altar' in the varying succession of Christian Festivals."

NOTES AND SOURCES

1) All this material is taken from the Balliol MS. Except the account of Oakeley,s view of Catholics at Lichfield which is to be found *in The Catholic Church before and after conversion* delivered as a Popular lecture in 1855. Printed and Published in that year. The material on Charles Sumner is taken from the *Life of Bishop Charles Sumner* by George Henry Sumner (London 1876) Page 45ff.
2) Based on the entry for Oakeley in Dictionary of National Biography
3) The account of his early days at Oxford is taken from *Reminiscences of Oxford and Oxford Men* selected by Lillian Quiller Couch. Vol 22 page 63ff. Published by the Oxford Historical Society in 1895. This memoir first appeared in the MONTH in Volumes 3 and 4 (1865-1866).
4) *Historicial Notes on the Tractarian Movement* by Frederick Oakeley published London 1865.
5) *Historical Notes* page 12 for the death of Lloyd.
6) Thomas Mozley- *Reminiscences Chiefly of Oriel and the Oxford Movement* 2 Vols (1882). The Ref. is Vol 2 page 228.
7) Newman, *Letters and Diaries*.Newman to Pusey 10 Jan 1837 L.D.Vol 6 Page 10
8) From the Balliol Manuscript Memoir.
9) *W.G.Ward and the Oxford Movement* The description of Ward and Oakeley as like "Castor and Pollox" etc is on Page 120. The description of the Common Room at Balliol on page 122.
10) *History of All Saints Margaret St.* Chapter l. [Seen by courtesy of the Custodian at the Church]
11) A description of the Chapel as Oakeley found it is to be found in *Historical Notes on the Tractarian Movement* page 58ff and also in Memorials of Mr Sergeant Bellasis by Edward Bellasis (London 1923 (3rd Ed). Page 40ff.

12) *Historical Notes on the Tractarian Movement* page 63 for the Cat.
13) *Contemporary Magazine* July 1874
14) *Things Dispensable and Things Indespensable. The Importance of distinguishing between them.* Two Sermons preached on the 10th and 17th November 1844 and printed in that year. This is from the first of the two sermons.
15) op.cit. The Second of the two sermons.
16) Bellasis *Memorials* page 42.
17) Pamphlet *To Hold as distinct from Teaching.* An open letter to his friends in the Church of England. (Published 25 June 1845)
18) The Judgement of Judge Fust is given in the TABLET July 5th 1845 on page 417. The description of the Court of Arches is taken from *Good and Faithful Servants* (The vicars of All Saints Margaret Street) by Peter Galloway and Christopher Rawll. (Page 3)
19) Information taken from *Rev J.E. Tenison Woods* (1832 to 1889) Pamphlet published privately in Canberra 1995.
20) Westminster Archdiocesan Archives. Wiseman Letters.
21) Mozley *Reminiscences* Vol 2. Page 5.
22) The full Reference is Brit Lib. GL 44, 127(184/185). It is quoted by R.W. Church and other authors writing on the Oxford Movement.
23) Funeral Oration given by Cardinal Manning. TABLET Sat Feb 7th 188 Page 179.

A Full list of Oakeley's printed Works is to be found in Gillow, *Biographies of English Catholics.*

A large number of his letters are to be found in the Bodleian Library at Oxford. Ref. Summary Catalogue of Post Medieval Western MSS in the Bodleian Library 1991. A particularly interesting selection can be found in MSS Wilberforce,C 7. "Letters to Wilberforce" (full refs from Summary Catalogue Vol 2 page 1373. His prize essays are printed in "Oxford English Prize Essays" (Oxford 2nd Edition 1836).

PART THREE
Richard Waldo Sibthorp
Looking both ways at once

Introduction.

Unlike Oakeley, the life of Sibthorp is quite well documented. A short time after his death a biography appeared written by an Anglican friend, Rev.J.Fowler. This gives an outline of his life written entirely from an Anglican perspective. However it consists mainly of a series of letters he wrote, and most of these were to his close friend since Oxford days, the Anglican Divine, John Rouse Bloxham. Bloxham was also a friend of Newman and the latter always prayed for his eventual conversion. Bloxham in turn is best remembered for his monumental work on the History of Magdalen College and the lives of its former members. Naturally Sibthorp has an honoured place in this list.

In 1938 R.D. Middleton wrote a substantial memoir is his book *Magdalen Studies* and later in 1953 Christopher Sykes made a study of Sibthorp in his work *Two Studies in Virtue*. A full collection of his works can be found in the Library of Magdalen college together with some letters which are included in the Bloxham collection. I include him in this collection of converts because he represents one of a small band of converts who wavered in their allegiance to their new faith after conversion. Technically he died as a Catholic Priest but I hope to show here that he probably never really understood the Catholic faith fully

CHAPTER ONE
Early Years.

Richard Waldo Sibthorp was born at Lincoln on the 4th October 1792. He was the youngest of the five children of Colonel Humphrey Sibthorp and his wife Sussanah Ellison formerly of Thorne near York. The Sibthorp family had resided for a long time in Lincoln and also had a long standing connection with Magdalen College Oxford. Richard's grandfather was Dr Humphrey Sibthorp who in 1847 became the Sheradian Professor of Biology at Oxford and during the 36 years he occupied that chair, is said to have only delivered one lecture and that not a successful one [1]. Richard's brother Charles was a well known eccentric Member of Parliament for Lincoln and colonel of militia.

His appearance was extraordinary and frequently caricatured; his speeches at times brutal and often given in a slovenly maaner. He opposed nearly everything including Catholic Emancipation, the Reform Bill and Free Trade.

The youngest son, Richard was a particular favorite of his mother who it appears was a formidable lady ruling the estate on an equal footing with her husband. When Richard was still an infant, the Sibthorp's employed a French Emigré Priest Fr William Beaumont as a tutor. He had been Rector of the University at Caen and Canon of Rouen Cathedral. When he refused to take the oath at the time of the French Revolution he was banished to England. Col. Sibthorp had met him earlier in Germany and now invited him to come and teach French and Latin to his children. Later he obtained for him the post of Catholic Missioner at Lincoln. In 1798, Beaumont had been responsible for the conversion of Henry Best following a conversation on belief in the real presence[2].

Although Beaumont did not tutor Richard Sibthorp it seems he was employed to teach him French during the holidays. Beaumont made no effort to convert the children as this was forbidden by the terms of his employment, but it seems that while still very young Richard was found kneeling saying his prayers before a crucifix, a thing unheard of at that time in Protestant circles. It is related that William Wilberforce, a friend of the family, said on hearing the news, "That boy will become a Roman Catholic".

As a young boy he was sent as a pupil to a private school run by the curate of Eltham, Kent, one John Smith, who had a good reputation for learning. Sibthorp enjoyed his time there and kept up correspondence with the family until he died. He then spent a couple of years at Westminster School where one of his fellow pupils was Dr. Longley, later head of Harrow and later still Archbishop of Canterbury. Again Sibthorp had a high regard for Longley but not for Westminster where on his own admission he "played the fool". As a result he was sent for a year to a private tutor to be prepared for entry into Magdalen College. His first attempt was unsuccessful and he matriculated at University College. However in 1810 he secured a demyship and entered the college so favoured by his family.

The principle of this college was the venerable figure of Dr. Martin Routh who had become principal in 1792 and remained there till his death 62 years later. He was well known for deep piety and hatred of Popery.

It seems that even from the beginning of his time at Oxford, Sibthorp had been slipping quietly off to the Catholic Chapel of St Clement's to hear Mass. Once again he had a crucifix in his room. He started to correspond with a Fr. Francis Martyn at Bloxwich. Martyn was the first priest to be entirely educated in England after the days of persecution were over and Catholics were free to open schools again.

It seems that he had been reading a book by Bishop Milner entitled *The End of Controversy* which contains a fine expose of the Catholic Faith. Later St.George Mivart would claim the same book influenced him in his journey towards Catholicism. Milner was Vicar Apostolic for the Western District and a somewhat eccentric character. He had no sense of humour and could not understand jokes. Unlike most Catholics he had no love of ritual and his crozier consisted of a metal hook rammed on to his walking stick.He was however a valiant fighter for Catholic Emancipation and in particular that when Emancipation came, there should be no conditions attached to the grant.

Shortly after the start of the term in October 1811

Sibthorp disappeared from Oxford and for a few days no one knew where he was.

His brother Coningsby came over to find out and after a short while discovered from a friend that his brother had gone to Bloxwich to be with Fr.Martyn. Taking with him a constable, Coningsby went in pursuit. On arrrival at Bloxwich, they were told that both Martyn and Sibthorp had left for the residence of Dr.Milner at Wolverhampton.

On arrival at Wolverhampton, the party knocked at the door and on its being opened made forcible entry, seized poor Sibthorp and took him back to Oxford. He had passed two nights there and was on the point of being received into the Church.

He was removed from Oxford for a few months in order to clear his mind of Popish thoughts. Mr Smith of Eltham was entrusted with this task which was successfully accomplished and he returned to Oxford to complete his education . He gained an Upper 2nd in 1813 and moved straight on to prepare for the ministry. Ordained Deacon in 1815 he was appointed curate at Waddington with Harmston near Lincoln. His sermons drew crowds right from the start. Driven by evangelical enthusiasm he overstepped the mark and would preach in private houses and in churches where he had no license to preach. The story that he preached in barns is probably untrue but it is certain that even at this very early date he was speaking of the Church of Christ as one entire whole from the Apostolic times to the present times. The implication was that he was not opposed to the Church of Rome.

In 1818 he was ordained priest but then had to defend himself to Routh in order to ensure that he would obtain the fellowship he desired. He affirmed that he did indeed hold the doctrine of the Church of England and on that affirmation he was appointed probationary fellow in July of that year and a full fellow the following year.

In 1817 he was appointed to a temporary curacy in Hull where he seems to have made a big impression. There is a printed version of a sermon of his preached on May

19th 1818. It has a strong evangelical flavour. Speaking of Justification by Faith he told his listeners that those who oppose this doctrine "rear up in its stead the merits of man, destroying the peace and comfort and hope of the humble Christian believer and in fact sapping that very morality which can only be acceptable to God when it springs from a pure and lively faith."[3]

In 1818 he took his first rectorship, at Tattershall in Lincolnshire. To make sure the inhabitants were well prepared for his arrival he had printed *An Address to the Inhabitants of Tattershall in Lincolnshire on Entering upon the Living of the Parish* He was giving them an outline of his methods and approach to the work. What he said about late arriving for services would surely hold good today in any Church.

"A Common and lamentable error by which not only they that are guilty of it, deprive themselves of joining in some of the most solemn and affecting parts of the liturgy and hasten in to the presence of God in a hurried, indecent and often careless manner; but the rest of the congregation are almost unavoidably disturbed in their devotions to say nothing of the bad example afforded to the younger part of the assemblly and the interruption given to the minister."[4]

In the text of the short life of Sibthorp prepared by Bloxham in his work on the demies of Magdalen, Bloxham gives an idea of one of the sermons he preached on the devil:

"Nothing could be more terrific than the picture which he drew of the ceaseless activity of the dread accuser - of the joy with which he beheld man fall into error - of the delight with which he presented every ommission of duty, and every commission of sin....of the diligence with which he prompts the recording angel to enter in the great book of account, the crimes, follies and omissions of every hour, or the exultation with which this task of perpetual accusation is carried on, and of the rapture with which its success is contemplated."

He spent several quiet years at Tattershall but after a

while found that it was too small a charge for his longing for ceaseless activity.

He left in 1825 and moved to London. There now followed a very intense period of work both there and later in Oxford. First he took over an evangelical Chapel known as the Percy Chapel at St Pancras and then in 1828 assisted Rev John Baptism Noel, an Irvingite, at the St John's Chapel, Bedford Row. However his ministrations were clouded by ill health. His mother died in 1826 in his arms. The circumstances were strange. Although his mother was in a decline, her death was not apparently imminent. Richard was staying with his mother and went out for a walk. He spoke of having an impression saying to him. "Go home directly!" He was met at the door by the maid who indicated his mother was dying and entering the living room found her collapsed on the sofa. Sibthorp relates "She was breathing her last, conscious and able to reply to my single question, 'Is Christ precious to you?' 'Yes; he is my only stay' and all was over."

He developed a fever which seems to have returned intermittently especially if he overworked himself over the next few years. For instance he had periods of great depression, especially as he tells us after preaching about the evils of Satan. It was also a time when he went through an intensely anti-Catholic period. One of his sermons at Bedford Row was printed. It is dated March 11th 1828. There is a particularly vicious attack on the institution of the Papacy for claming virtually Divine Rights and a specific attack on the process and ritual of the canonisation of Saints. He called this "Making a creature to be worshipped and prayed to as a sort of demi-God by the faithful on earth; a decision which if erroneous, involves all in idolatry."[5]

When his Doctor told him that if he carried on the way he was going with this type of preaching his mind would give way, he replied "Then I will die on the pulpit steps".

Although he continued to attract good crowds and

many of his sermons were printed, he decided to return to Oxford. The reasons for his move are obscure but one factor was certainly a hope that he might become the vice-President of his old college. In this he was to be disappointed. However he took up his fellowship and made the acquaintance of Newman through their membership of the Church Missionary Society, especially in Appeal Preaching. Eventually this extreme Evangelical group forced Newman to resign as secretary, but before that happened Sibthorp was involved in a dispute with Mr Bulteel who organised the preaching. The incident is related in Newman's Letters and Diaries [6] It seems that he preached that Christ died for all men and that Mr Bulteel felt obliged to get up that same afternoon and deny the truth of what his comrade was saying. At this time also he was in the habit of preaching at a small chapel at Kennington near Oxford. A frequent visitor to hear him preach was Gladstone who wrote to Sibthorp's biographer "I have nothing more of the Oxford Sibthorp than a soothing general recollection, a venerable visual image in the mind's eye and a moral certainty that the preaching was, at least of singular grace and charm which drew me again and again to walk some miles out of Oxford..." [7]

Failing to obtain the position he sought at Magdalen and seeing that he would never gain promotion in the Church, Sibthorp determined to settle at Lincoln and obtained a property there. But a shock was in store. The local residents had heard of his reputation and decided they did not want him however good a preacher he was. There was only one solution at present, to work once again in a proprietary chapel like Bedford Row (and like the Margaret Chapel where Oakeley worked). But what patron would take him on? Well that was not really a problem for one thing that Sibthorp was never short of was money.

Just at the right time for our subject the proprietary chapel of St.James at Ryde, in the Isle of Wight came on the market. It had only been opened in 1827 by a Mr Hughes Hughes, but this gentleman sold the chapel to Sibthorp on becoming Member of Parliament for Oxford.

Proprietary chapels were described by T.Francis Bumpus in his *London Churches Ancient and Modern* as:

> "Well pewed, well warmed, undedicated, unendowed, and unconsecrated; where captivating preachers of the morphine velvet, lavender kid glove school of theology dispensed the most comfortable doctrines. The pews were filled and the good promoters were amply repaid by the pious tenantry but accomodation for the poor was never thought of"[8]

Neither Margaret St, nor St. James Ryde fitted that description though, for both Oakeley and Sibthorp were excellent missioners who certainly did not neglect the poor.

Ryde was a growing town with about 3000 inhabitants at the time Sibthorp came there and already connected to the mainland by a steampacket service to Portsmouth.

The license to preach and conduct services was duly given by the Bishop of Winchester, Charles Sumner. The Church which could hold about 600 if jammed in, was improved by Sibthorp as soon as he arrived. His reputation had preceded him and the Church was packed out particularly in holiday times with folk from the mainland coming over even specially to hear him. Many of the nobility started keeping holiday homes on the Isle. These included the Duke of Buckingham, the Simeons, Earl Spencer and the Oakeley family who kept a house at Chale. Many of these attended the services when in town. We learn that officers from the navy ships at Portsmouth would come across, and that domestic staff were accomodated in the two galleries, menservants on one side and maids on the other! Once again he started printing his sermons or at least some of them. This time it was a series on the Book of Jonah.

To start with he lived in lodgings, then in a small house in town but from about 1834 he lived in a house he had specially built for him about one mile south of Ryde called 'Holmwood'. This house was pulled down about 1950 and a small estate is to be found there now.

About 1834 or 1835 a great change came over Sibthorp. Up till then he had been a thorough going Evangelical but now he was becoming a ritualist and changing his doctrinal approach. He introduced a boys choir clad in surplices. These boys were entirely cared for by Sibthorp at his own expense and most were lodged with him at Holmwood with a master to care for them. He also employed seven gardeners to look after his estate there. It might be well to point out at this stage that there was never any suggestion of impropriety made against him. Certainly he never married but he opted for the celibate state in much the same way as a Catholic Priest would, as a means of serving Almighty God the better.

The new approach seems to have started after he had heard a sermon from Samuel Wilberforce (Soapy Sam) at a clerical meeting. Henry Wilberforce wrote to Newman on 30th November 1836

> " I told you three years ago he heard a very full exposition of the doctrine of Baptism from Sam at a clerical meeting and seemed much inclined to adopt it...he has gone on regularly and is now preaching the Succession, the superiority of the Church Prayers to preaching and that he will not say that those who are out of the church cannot be saved because he leaves that to God etc. Last week at a clerical meeting he avowed his approval of prayers for the dead and renounced the evangelical view of justification by faith saying that Wesley had done great harm by making people look for their personal comfort etc to their own feelings etc instead of to their Baptism, and that the Evangelical Clergy had fallen into the same...All this under God is Sam's doing...The Evangelicals of Ryde are furious. They say they took their houses to be near Sibthorp." (9)

There were other factors at work also. Sibthorp took to making frequent visits to Oxford to see Routh and met there a young demi soon to be a fellow, John Rouse Bloxham. Bloxham was already imbued with the spirit of the Tractarians and they became close friends, remaining so through thick and thin all the remainder of their lives. As

Bloxham was also very close to Newman even though he never became a Catholic Newman would have been informed about all Sibthorp's movements.

The evidence of Newman's Letters and diaries for the period 1835 to 1840 suggests several meetings and exchange of letters. In 1838 Newman refers to the idea mooted by Sibthorp of a Breviary in English.

What one can safely say is that he was most certainly affected greatly by the Tractarian movement. What then of other factors ?

We know that he started seeing the Catholic Priest at Cowes and discussing Church unity with him. It would seem too that this Priest persuaded him that his orders were not valid. A few details have come down to us of his style of service in the latter days at Ryde. One gentleman relates that his sermons were long, he could not stop preaching, he saw no way of stopping ! Another writer tells us that the morning service lasted three hours with the organ playing one hour of that time. Someone who came to an evening service related that the organ played 33 times during the course of the proceedings, while another considered Mr Sibthorp was a "good man in a fit of insanity" (10)

One friend who visited him just before he left Ryde was the famous architect Augustus Welby Pugin who may have been a distant relative as it seems he always called Sibthorp 'Cousin'. He was not over impressed. Writing to Bloxham he said "I think his intentions are truly admirable but to speak the truth the Sanctuary looks amazingly like one of the modern Catholic Chapels; there is too much finery to produce the solemn effect."

Then suddenly almost like a bolt from the blue he left Ryde and became a Catholic. At the end of October 1841 he arrived at Oxford and consulted with Bloxham with a view to a meeting with Bishop Wiseman at Oscott. There was a final meeting with Newman first, most likely in Bloxham's rooms. According to one account Sibthorp announced "I am going to Oscott". Newman replied "Mind you do not stop there". In Newman's own account which he related to Fowler he said that he had tried to dissuade him. "I did all I could without rudeness to show my dislike of him going to Oxford and as we rose from the table in Bloxham's rooms I asked him where he was going and he said "to Oscott" and there was a general laugh as if it meant 'to Rome' on which he exclaimed 'Oh, I have no such intention you need not be afraid' or some such words."

However his mind was made up already. He went on to Oscott where the next day, the 27th October 1841 he became a Roman Catholic.

PART TWO.

To Rome and Back to Rome.

A few days later Sibthorp returned to Oxford looking worn and agitated and announced to everyone that he was now a Catholic. He called on Newman to try and effect his conversion but Newman related to Fowler that "he only threw me back by the methodistical character as I felt them to be, of the reasons he gave for the step which he had taken."

Sibthorp meanwhile returned to the Isle of Wight and made arrangments for the sale of the House and of the Church which was re-purchased by Mr Hughes and returned to its accustomed evangelical style. The former Rector then went off to spend the next few months preparing to become a Catholic Priest.

Sibthorp was attacked almost brutally by his former colleagues for his actions and was left to defend himself in the traditional form of the day, the open letter in pamphlet form. This time the pamphlets went flying backwards and forwards. It is certainly necessary in order to understand his mind to look at the arguments but I am of the opinion that the real reason for his conversion was his desire for Church unity which had been encouraged by the Catholic Priest at Ryde who told him of the interest shown in this work by Fr. Ignatius Spencer then at Oscott, and later to become a Passionist Priest.

On Founders Day at St Mary Magdalen's on the Feast of St Mark he had preached the official sermon and the topic was Church unity. In the course of his discourse he said:

> "There is little true unity in the Church and therefore small blessing of God on her effects - Satan Triumphs, Christ is failed, Christianity is dishonoured...let each of us as far as we can, seek after Christian Unity." (ll)

The remainder of the sermon is a very fine exposition of the doctrine of the Mystical Body of Christ based on St. Paul's teachings.

After reading the text I would find it amazing that anyone present would be surprised if the preacher did not soon turn to Rome.

Sibthorp however was pressed to defend himself by none other than Dodsworth. In his reply explaining his reasons he argues:

> "About five years since in the course of my ministry at Ryde, I was led to review the Jewish Economy or the Church under the New Testament dispensation. The subject came minutely under my notice while engaged in a series of lectures on the Levitical Law and institutions. It is universally admitted that they were typical of something better, 'of good things to come' from Israel viewed as a nation.. Where then was to be found this 'something better'? Where was the antitype of this typical dispensation? I naturally sought it in a careful comparison of the Christian dispensation with these types and I found one immediate answer to my enquiry, and full of holy and consolatry instruction. They had an accomplishment in Christ, as is largely shown by the Epistle to the Hebrews. He is the typified Temple and High Priest, and Victim. His blood and righteousness, mediation and intercession, his ministry, character and offices were prefigured by what went before....The types like most of the prophecies and psalms have a further application than to Christ personally or officially. But to whom or to what ? It is to His Mystical Body, the Church under the New Testament."

In his argument Sibthorp went on to describe how he

had considered that the Anglican Communion seemed to fit the idea of an organised body with two sacraments. But then he went back again to look at the Israelite model of the Church and discovered

"a compact and united body really and visibly united in all its parts, combining them in a most perfect and evident unity of faith or worship. Unity too of laws, discipline, religious ordinances and even of minute ceremonies; no variety permitted, no departure from the oneness demanded being sanctioned in any individual. Such was ancient Israel. If typical of the Church, such should be the Israel of God under the New Testament."

His argument continues in his search for such a body today, adding

"by a supreme spiritual rule in a succession of individuals by unbroken pastoral descent from...the apostles, by continued daily sacrifice, by a sevenfold channel of sacramental grace, illumined and illuminating all within her, by an impressive magnificent significant ritual....so that from north to south, from east to west, there should not be on earth one Christian that differed from another and wherever he journeyed over the wide earth, the same religion he left at home he should always find."

He continued his argument by saying

"I looked back to the primitive apostolic Church of the first six centuries and I found an exact correspondency with the type of the Catholic Church in communion with the see of Rome...the close and perfect antitype of the Church under the Old Testament."

A few other points can be made to illustrate his reasoning.

The seven sacraments (rather than the Anglican two) are to correspond with the seven fold light perpetually fed by the Holy Oil in the Temple. He argued that no one clergyman in ten thousand who subscribed to the 39 articles ever supposed them to be capable of a Catholic interpretation and speaking of the theory that the Catholic and Anglican Churches are two branches of the same Church he says:

> "I cannot see how this removes that objection to the visibility and perfection of the unity which must strike everyone as arising from the evident opposition of these two branches, in doctrine as well as discipline....If the Catholic Church in England from St Augustine's Day to the Reformation was a sound member of the mystical body of the Lord, of his visible Church, the modern Anglican is an unsound one; and if the latter be sound in her present doctrine and her rejection of the See of St Peter, the Catholic Church is to be regarded as most unsound. She is most unsound whether she be regarded at any time previous or subsequent to the 16th century; for she is the same now as then in doctrine and discipline".

Yet surely the clarity of his argument is destroyed when he writes (page 35)

> "I know not a Protestant controversial writer, the authors of the Oxford Tracts excepted, whose works did not leave me more a Catholic than before; while I admit there were some writings of Catholics which when I read them, threw me back upon Protestantism. It is foreign to my purpose in this letter to discuss these disputed tenets."

Surely if he was to impress his readers he should have tried to show what the so called disputed points which bothered him exactly were. Yet he goes on a little later to say:

> "I was once pressed with this principle, that a person was bound to remain in that Church in which the providence of God had placed him by his birth, baptism and and calling into the ministry".

His own life was hardly a good example of this principle yet in later life we find him at times asking others to accept it and not change their faith.[12]

Following a further attack on his position by Dodsworth and Palmer he wrote another "Open Letter" entitled *A further Answer to the Enquiry why have you become a Catholic..containing the notice of the strictures of the Rev. Messrs Palmer and Dodsworth upon a former letter.* This letter was issued from Oscott on Ash

Wednesday 1842, while the earlier letter was sent from Holmwood, Isle of Wight on the Feast of the Epiphany, and just before he sold the house there.

In this second letter he explains quite satisfactorily all the particular points of Catholic Doctrine except perhaps devotion to Our Lady. On this he writes:

"The doctrine of the Church is essentially the same as with the Saints. As a creature she possesses no divine attribute more than any other creature and is as much the redeemed of her Son and partaker of his salvation by Grace as any one of the Church triumphant."

He speaks of the special role of affection for Our Lady but mediation, atonement and special offices apply to Christ alone, while "in another sense that of intercession, her mediation is applicable to any one who pleads for others and in this sense only is the Blessed Virgin called, and that rarely, a mediatrix."

On that evidence he would hardly seem to believe in the doctrine of the Immaculate Conception leaving aside the question of Our Lady as Mediatrix of all Graces. As far as I can gather he rarely spoke of Our Blessed Lady in his sermons as a Catholic Priest either at this time or during his re-incarnation as a priest from the mid 1860's onwards.

Sibthorp seems to have left the Isle of Wight in January 1842 to study at Oscott for the Priestood. Here he would have come into close contact with Dr. Wiseman who personally conducted his studies and also with Fr. Ignatius Spencer. He was particularly attached to Spencer because of his great hopes for Christian Unity and they remained friends. Spencer always prayed for Sibthorp's recoversion following the defection of 1843.

Sibthorp was certainly given a very hurried prepartion. A course usually taking six years was condensed into less than six months.

He was made sub-deacon on February 19th 1842, Deacon on March 13th and ordained to the Priesthood at Oscott on May 21st. He was soon allowed to preach which he did wearing his Oxford Bachelor of Divinity Hood rather than a biretta!

He had great hopes of going to Nottingham where he interested himself in the building of the new Catholic Cathedral. However such hopes were ended when Wiseman sent him to Birmingham to St.Chad's, now the Cathedral Church of the present Archdiocese of Birmingham.

A brief spell living with the clergy there persuaded him that he would be better off on his own so he took a house and spent much time visiting the poor. In July he wrote to a friend. "I am still here but unsettled". He made no attempt to proselytise and told a lady who called about possible conversion that she should not leave the Church if she found peace where she was.

It would seem he was allowed to preach now and then even before his ordination to the priesthood as four days after he was ordained deacon he was in action at St. Chad's for St Patrick's Day, both in the morning and in the evening and these sermons were published.

Both cover the same ground; the way a Christian should conduct his life. Much stress is put on the importance of example. The tone of both sermons is fully Catholic. From the first sermon we hear:

> "...In the land in which you live, you are compelled to be a spectacle to angels, by being, as it were led forth, appointed to trials, to sufferings and in a conflict to death. For you are men against whom there is a peculiar degree of trial at work and unless you contend manfully for the faith delivered to the saints, your forefathers, it will be too much for you and you will give way to your ruin."

He goes on to make a strong attack on his late faith:

> "As men what do they think of the Church of Christ in this country? Is she deemed the Spouse of Christ?...doth the State manifest its highest glory to hold the stirrup for Christ's Spouse while she rides through the land in honour and triumph..? No not so! It is the very spirit of Protestantism to destroy the corporate character of the Church. Take away her corporate charactaer and you take away her dignity."

In the afternoon sermon he continued the good work:

> "I pray you to contribute to that glory, I pray you carry

away with you the important truth, that you are called to adorn the true spiritual real Church of Christ by holy consistent Catholic living. Walk watchfully, walk humbly, walk prayerfully, walk according to the rule of your Holy Church, the careful mother of her Children. She will guide you to heaven, both by precept and example if you will follow the pattern and the injunctions she sets before you. She has introduced you to the Church in Holy Baptism, she will carry you on through every stage of your course till she lands you safe in heavenly glory."

By August of 1842 the tone had distinctly changed. No more attacks on the Protestants, indeed nothing that could remotely upset them. In his sermon for the opening at St Oswald's in Liverpool on August 4th he speaks of salvation from aspects of hope, faith and catholicity with a small *c*.

"Take catholicity from the church and we trust to an indefinite principle." He goes on to describe this catholicity in history.

"History will show us how when she was brought low, she overcame every trial and when likely to be overtopped by the waves, she braved every storm and rose more beautiful than ever. When brought low by Pagan persecution she also came out more glorious than before. When she had overcome these, other persecutions arose in the person of Arius, and during this fiery ordeal she was reduced almost to a gasping state, but she came out of it with renewed beauty and vigour. In like manner when the Mohammedans spread desolation over her pastures in the time of her necessity, the Almighty stretched forth his hand and said to them". Thus far and no further "Next came heresies which compelled her to close her places of worship. History testifies to the things and shows how the church came out of these persecutions with strength renewed like the eagles."

In the whole sermon there is no mention of the word *Catholic* as opposed to *Catholicity*. The Protestant reformation is completely ignored and the solidity of the

Church is not based upon St Peter in any way but directly on Christ. "When then I see the solidity of this Church, and that its foundations are built upon Christ, am I not justified in saying, and there is scripture for the fact, that the Church or Kingdom of Christ shall last for ever."

The same muddle and confusion is exhibited in a sermon preached at Lincoln Catholic Church on September 19th 1842. This is reported in the *London and Dublin Orthodox Journal* Vol XV no 378. He was preaching about the infinite variety of sects which were creating dissension in the Christian world and contrasting this with the desire to realise on earth what can only exist in heaven, *a really Catholic Church*. (Ie. Not *THE* Catholic Church but *A* Catholic Church.) He remarked that "Universality of Opinion never did and never will exist under any circumstances; and towards producing it preaching and penal enactments have failed as completely as would endeavour to chain lightning." Yet by the end of his sermon he was saying almost the opposite. The reporter relates that he emphatically pronounced that the day of Catholicism (with a big *C*) was dawning.

In October of 1842 Sibthorp met with a serious accident. While at Skipton in Yorkshire he had a fall from a carriage and his spine and the back of his head were injured. Wiseman writing to Lord Shreswbury after Sibthorp had reverted to Anglicanism wrote that the fall "..had hurt his mental powers. We who were in intercourse with him observed it then most painfully. He was never the same man at all after." [13]

This is an unlikely explanation of his reversion. Perhaps Bishop Wilberforce writing to Charles Anderson in 1841 was already nearer the mark when he said:

> "Poor Sibthorp, his head was as you know never a sound one...He had exposed himself to temptation by long formed habits of grievous self will in religious matters, breaking out in his low church excesses.."

Newman agreed with this view in a letter to Bloxham

of April 12th 1881:

> "He had a hundred good and high qualities, was devout, single minded and kind hearted but what spoke him to my mind, (may I say it without offence) is the perpetual I I I throughout his letters. If he would forget himself and cease to remind his readers of his own central position his letters would be charming." (14)

Soon after this injury letters appeared in the Papers attacking the recent convert. First in *The Times* for the 10th and 13th November he was accused of revolutionary leanings in his politics and in attempting to sell his Church of St. James to a catholic purchaser while still an Anglican Minister.

Worse was to follow. At the start of 1843 he dined with Routh in his rooms at Magdalen although of course he had been struck the list of fellows. This in turn led to a report in the *Morning Star* that he was about to return to the Anglican fold. Wiseman then wrote to that paper as follows:

> "My attention has been called to a paragraph in which it is stated the Mr S. is reported to have already serious differences with his brethren of the Romish priesthood; thus he refuses to pray to the virgin or to be a party to auricular confession, that an appeal is now pending to Rome...and should the decision be adverse, Mr S, it is said, will secede from the Romish church. Had there been the slightest ground for any one of the statements put forth in that paragraph I must from my position have been acquainted with it, and Mr S, whom I have seen this very evening, is aware of my intention of writing this contradiction"

Sibthorp also wrote to the *Tablet* to defend himself but his letter gives rise to the impression that he has failed to grasp the fullness of Catholic Doctrine about Our Lady:

> "Assuredly I do not WORSHIP her, but neither does the Catholic Church require me to worship her or any but God...It is foolish to accuse me of disapproving of auricular or private confession when the Protestant Church of England at least commends it on some and frequent occasions." (15)

During the first half of 1843 he continued at

Birmingham but more and more in an unsettled frame of mind. Finally in June of that year he left for the Isle of Wight and took a cottage at St Helen's near Ryde to which was attached an oratory in which he said Mass for the benefit of local Catholics.

His final move back to the Anglican fold was prompted at least in part by an unfortunate accident. His acolyte entrusted with the duty of putting out the candles in the oratory failed one day to do so and the room caught fire destroying versments, pictures altar linens etc.

It was just the kind of "warning from God" that Sibthorp always looked for. It so happened that at the start of 1842 he had been staying with Kenelm Digby at his house in Southampton when the house there had been burnt down. In that case it was almost certainly an act of arson prompted by the sad fact that at a local dissenters chapel two days earlier, the minister who knew of Sibthorp's presence in town said to his congreation "That man should be burned!" One can therefore imagine Sibthorp recalling that incident and deciding he had made a bad choice in moving over to Rome.(16)

On October 2nd he wrote to Routh at Magdalen College informing him that he had the previous day taken communion at the local Anglican Church and hoped to receive Communion at Magdalen if that was not judged to be improper.

When Wiseman heard the news it is reported that he took to his bed with shock for the remainder of the day. His Anglican friends were at first not certain what to think. J.B.Mozley relates that in a letter from Bloxham the latter indicated that it was "Mariolatry, the point on which he has started" (ie reverted to Anglicanism).(17)

To ensure that his friends believed his change of heart was permanent he wrote to Routh in March:

> "I request that my name be replaced at your discretion on the books of Magdalen College...I wish I could wipe out those two years and a half and recall a step which was hastily taken under the strain of a strong and excited feeling." (18)

There is one letter of this period in which he uses strong language about Rome reminiscent of his days in London but it is a single reference in dozens of letters. Indeed writing in November from St Helen's he says to Routh:

"I wish to assure you I am aiming to live prostrate at God's disposal; I still praise, and unless I come to see things very differently, shall praise the Catholic Church for her daily devotions, her hourly offices, her symbolic rites, her inestimable practice of confession, her intercommunion with the spirits of the just made perfect."

All this remember from one who had supposedly just rejoined the Anglican Church. Certainly at this moment he was a mass of contradictions. In the offensive letter written to an Anglican cleric called Bickersteth he had written:

"The conviction I am come to after most painful deliberation is that the Church of Rome is the Harlot and Babylon in the Apocalypse."(19)

Sibthorp was not permitted to practice as an Anglican minister until he could obtain the Bishop's license. The Bishop was Charles Sumner and he viewed Sibthorp with the greatest suspicion. He told him that he would have to live for three years at Winchester itself and show himself to be a good and practising member of the Anglican Communion. Sibthorp complied and moved to Winchester. At the end of the three year period he again applied for a license only to find Sumner still seeking to impose conditions. This time he asked for a written undertaking that Sibthorp accepted fully the Protestant doctrine on certain matters which were disputed by Catholics. It seems that Sumner had heard from a Catholic Priest, that Sibthorp had been seen attending Catholic Churches in London. Sibthorp was so irritated he withdrew his application and decided to return to his home territory of Lincoln. Here the Bishop was far more amenable and did not require a public recantation but merely a statement which need not be made public. To this Sibthorp agreed and was readmitted as a minister of the Anglican Communion on the 23rd December 1847.

Always thoughtful of the poor, he decided to reinstate a medieval custom and build some special alms houses known as Bedes Houses where the inmates could live out their days in retirement with the special requirement that they attend the Anglican service regularly. So the St Anne's Bedes Houses which still stand in Lincoln, were built by George Myers, the regular builder to Pugin and using plans drawn up by the great architect. Sibthorp settled himself in a small house next to the houses and acted as chaplain in addition to local preaching as and when required. His rehabilitation as an Anglican was completed in 1848 when he was re-instated on the college lists at Magdalen.

This period of his life was very quiet. He became quite an important figure in the Church life of Lincoln, seeming to many a man surrounded indeed by others yet alone with God. He breathed an atmosphere of prayer. He was a friend to many families in the town and was often called to the bedsides of the sick and dying. At the same time judging from his letters he was really rather depressed as he had less opportunity of seeing his old friends. At times he seems quite despondent and always unsettled. In matters of religion he developed a strong dislike for the works of Fr. Faber. In particular he found the life of St.Philip Neri most distasteful. He regarded much of Faber's writing as the gloryfying of superstition. Almost at the same time as will be shown later, Richard Simpson was holding almost exactly the same views as Sibthorp about Faber.

He certainly maintained some Catholic contacts during his time at Lincoln. We know that Fr.Ignatius Spencer used to visit him now and then. He visited St Chad's Birmingham in 1849 and was kindly received by the brethren. Just after this he wrote:

"All modern converts have thrown themselves heart and soul into the ultra-dogmatic party which now includes nine tenths of the Church of Rome. Her priests and people are no longer cognisant of the distinction truly existing between the Ante-Tridentine Church and the modern Church of Rome." [20]

Here we see the start of hostility to the Papal claims. Eventually this would lead him to reject Papal Infallibility though he failed to do the logical thing and join the Old Catholics after 1870. His religious position in the 1850s was fast becoming what he would call "real old catholic" rather than Papal and he was already developing his own theory of the Church which might be called the "twig" theory, a special variety of the "branch theory" whereby the Anglican Church and the Catholic Church (pre-Tridentine as he saw it) were two twigs on the same branch. Though he would revert to being a Catholic priest, his basic theological position was set in 1849 and never really altered.

Sibthorp continued to minister to his Bedesmen until the Summer of 1864. He then handed over the pastoral care to his assistant and later biographer Mr Fowler and at the end of the year betook himself to London where he started attending Mass at the Carmelite Church in Kensington. On Jan 8th 1865 he was received back into the Catholic Church and immediately re-instated as a Catholic Priest.

CHAPTER FOUR.

Apriest Again. Final Years and Death.

What then had sparked off this re-conversion ? His biogaphers all point to two decisive works that he had just read. At the end of 1863 or the start of 1864 he read the Abbe Monin's *Life of the Cure d'Ars.*

At first sight it seems remarkable that such a work could have had any effect on him at all other than to regard it in the same way as the life of St Philip Neri. Here was a Saint who worked many miracles, whose main work was the hearing of confessions (for which it was alleged Sibthorp saw little use). Here was a simple country priest working amongst simple country people, far removed from the elegance of Oxford. No, what him impressed him most was the simple evangelical flavour of his preaching coupled with his evident love of the poor and humbleness of life.

Newman's *Apologia* appeared in instalments and it seems Sibthorp awaited each instalment with great eagerness. Not only did it recall for him the life at Oxford, but he saw Newman as a kind of bridge between Catholicism and Anglicanism, and as an upholder of all that was best in the Christian tradition in general.

There were other influences at work. During 1864 he visited the Redemptorists at Clapham to see an old friend George Yard who was preparing for ordination. He was deeply impressed by what he saw. This was reinforced all the more by the realisation that it was in their very house that once

"old Mr Wilberforce used to play at tilt and tournament with his sons - the present Bishop of Oxford and three who joined the Church of Rome."

He describes the Redemptorists as giving instructions three or four times a day, while others visit in the streets and alleys and sit in the confessional "till 12 at night for those who may be in various ways moved by their instructions." He considered that *this* is the way to get at the London masses.

"They must be ferretted out and won over to think of God and his goodness, and Death, Heaven and Hell, by services and teaching adapted to their ignorance and need of external application to their senses. The Church of England with her long calm, high-toned, and refined morning and evening services, and sermons often addressed more to the intellect than to the heart, the sermons of gentlemen and scholars, touches them not."

Finally Bloxham himself left in his collection of Sibthorp material at Magdalen a note extracted from the "Life of Hon.George Spencer, (Fr. Ignatius) (Dublin 1864) We read there that:

"He (Spencer) always hoped for his return to the Catholic Faith and strange enough, one of the first pieces of news in the way of conversion which we heard after Fr. Ignatius Death, (Sept 25th 1864), was his return to the faith which he had deserted."

It is interesting to note also that after Sibthorp's defection Spencer wrote to Newman and his companions then at Littlemore to say a novena of prayers for his eventual return. Perhaps we can say that it was the intercession of the Curé d'Ars, coupled with that of Fr. Ignatius Spencer which won for Sibthorp the grace of conversion.

When he came to be re-admitted to the priesthood Cardinal Wiseman lay dying but he arranged to have his bed taken downstairs and placed in his parlour which was next to the private oratory in which he used to say Mass. In this way he was able to assist at the first Mass said by the returning prodigal son. He died three weeks later.

After his re-conversion, Sibthorp set off to visit his old Catholic friends. He visited Birmingham and Oscott. At the Oratory he met with Newman for the first time since he had left the Isle of Wight. Newman told him that he ought to go at once to Lincoln and offer Mass in the little chapel there that had once been used many years ago by the Abbe Beaumont. Sibthorp complied at once with this advice. There was then the question of his future employment. He was over 70 but felt that he could still be of use. The Bishop of Nottingham offered him the chance to minister to the people in the Cathedral Parish. It seems that some years before Sibthorp had contributed £2,000.00 towards the building of the Cathedral, an enormous figure in terms of todays values. After a few changes of address he finally settled in a comfortable house very close to the Cathedral. He remained on the official list of active clergy for about six years, but even when the Catholic Directory listed him as 'retired' he still continued to say Mass publicly and help out when he could. He even heard confessions, perhaps at last persuaded by the influence of the Curé d'Ars.

He was present for the consecration of Cardinal Manning and wrote to Mr Fowler about the event. His description of Manning's appearance must be reckoned as one of the great religious quotes of the century.

> "He looked like Lazarus come out of the tomb in cope and mitre - a richly vested corpse but very dignified and placid."

He remarks too on the presence of Dr. Newman:

> "I just saw him to shake hands with him. As his manner is he kept retired, but had come up for the ceremony and immediately afterwards was seen in the sacristy on his knees before the Archbishop, who hastened to raise him up and embrace him." [21]

Soon he settled down to a routine at the Cathedral. He describes his life through the letters to Fowler and Bloxham which were published by Fowler in the Biography after his death.

On Good Friday he relates in a letter to Bloxham

"Our choir, one of the best I know, twelve or fourteen men, some boys, and two or three females in the background out of sight; music well selected." He goes on to mention a problem which seemed to affect him somewhat:

> "What is to be the upshot and end of the vestment controversy ?"

It seems that Nottingham had decided to abandon their gothic style vestments in favour of the Roman style. We find Sibthorp writing,

> "All the surplices have been cut up into cottas- frightful things like bibs, not reaching even to the hips. I hold on to my little surplice which therefore has escaped the massacre."

During his years at Nottingham Cathedral he always urged as one might expect from an old evangelical, that his parishioners should read the Bible. He was also anxious to reform the rite of Mass it seems. What he was thinking of was to blend together the best parts of the Roman Missal and Anglican Prayer to create a new service book that might suit the members of both Churches.

He enjoyed writing long letters to his friends which are often quite amusing, and at the same time a useful guide to his religious thinking. Sometimes they pass from the ridiculous to the sublime. For instance on August 25th 1873 he wrote a very long letter to an old parishioner at Ryde. He starts off with his views about Oxford University as it was then.

> "Discipline is nearly extinct, cricket, athletic sports and boating are uppermost. And that annual boat race in London injures very many very seriously! I wonder the two universities permit it, if it has not gone too far it should be stopped." [He goes on to speak of his own sporting activities:] "I take occasional recreation in a game of bowls. Nottingham is a great place for bowls. I find the exercise in the open air on a breezy hill, and the interest of the game really benefits me." [But then the mood changes; he goes on to enter on a meditation on the Kingdom of God:]
>
> "..What is..the purpose of God in the Redemption of the world; and of Christ's coming, and return to Heaven, to get to Himself a Kingdom. It is far more than a visible Church. It is man himself - a creature of various and marvellous faculties and really great powers, a little lower only than the higher order of creatures, the angels. To possess this His creature for Himself - this is Christianity in its present aim. How little understood! How much forgot! How feebly realised!. What less can we understand the Apostle to mean by 'To me to live is Christ' and again 'Not I, but Christ liveth in me'..? Prayer only, much true prayer, leading us to realise the Immensity of God, in some feeble measure; and to get somewhat absorbed in and into God.....And this apprehension and this likeness are a gradual work of God by the Holy Spirit, in and on man; in his affections, faculties, every power, and his whole being and life."[22]

We have only one sermon in printed form for the Nottingham Years.

It is for New Years Day 1867. It is at least slightly less gloomy than many of his earlier works. It is based on the theme "The Eternal Years" and considers naturally that each new year brings us closer to the Kingdom of God.

"The world is now keeping holiday as well as we. What is it for? A new term of existence is coming round, and it hopes either for a continuance of the blessings and pleasures it now enjoys, or that the coming year will bring greater or additional ones. I know of no other reason, and yet if this is all, how unworthy a subject of joy for souls that are immortal! Still, even natural hope is a blessed gift of God and one to be truly grateful for. Indeed without it, life would be intolerable. It keeps up the heart of man, so easily despondent with the fair promises even in things of this world.....Of the past year, the simply wordly and sensual man takes no further thought. It brought him his share of pleasures and he enjoyed them. It brought him sorrows too, but he has survived them. In his view the year is dead and buried, and his relationship with it is dissolved for ever. So he thinks! Ah he little dreams how those years of his will rise to meet him the day of judgement! They will stand to witness for or against him at the bar of God....And Eternity what does the world think of this ? Alas, it knows little about it and cares less. It is an unknown land into the mysteries of which it has never penetrated...How different is the Happy New Year of the Christian! He welcomes the new year as another friend who is come to lead him on his journey home. The old year was a dear old friend which lived its day, and brought him special blessings and his grateful soul will not soon forget them. Mercy has turned the course of his life from evil to good. It has changed the siner's fear of punishment into the confiding love of the devoted child. It has laid up treasure for him the 'Eternal Years'"

Sibthorp goes on to give examples of those who lives have changed over the year and then comes a passage which might apply to himself but only to a limited extent!

"Wish this man too a Happy New Year. This day a year ago he was outside the fold of Christ. Much as he longed for the possession of truth, he had not found it. He was in an unhappy state of doubt. He roamed about seeking rest for his uneasy conscience, but found none. But today he is a child of Holy Church...Those glorious old truths, which yet are ever new, have become his strength and joy. The clouds of doubt have passed away and all is open blue sky..."

He closes his homily with this words:

"Think often on the 'Eternal Years' The thought is the very balance wheel of life. It will keep the rich, and naturally gifted from pride's vain glory. It will lift up the poor and lowly in this world's estimation, from the dangers of discouragement. And now my dearest brethren, you understand my full meaning when, with these eternal years in view, I join with all your friends and well wishers this morning to wish you a 'Happy New Year'."

In 1876 Manning came to visit Nottingham and Sibthorp came to see him. He was given a warm welcome and they spoke of Oxford days and men. Indeed so well did they get on that Manning returned the compliment by calling on Sibthorp the very next day. However it would seem that after 1865 he never saw Newman again. It was not a case of ceasing a relationship but merely a kind of correspondence lapsing for right up until just before he died Sibthorp looked on Newman as the bridge between Catholicism and Anglicanism.

The last couple of years of his life were taken up with the writing of a book of meditations entitled *Daily Bread.* This appeared in two forms. The first was issued two years before he died and was entitled *A few meditations for the use of Catholic Christians* and carried the imprimatur of the Bishop of Nottingham. It uses the Douay version of Holy Scripture and is said to be adapted from sermons delivered at St Barnabas Cathedral. There are 162 sermonettes in a total of 167 pages and the main emphasis is on fallen mankind, temptations, the crucifixion, and self denial. Not exactly a work to cheer one up.

The 2nd edition was published after Sibthorp's death. This time there are 358 meditations spread over 726 pages and the old meditations have been completely re-written. Some have versicles attached. In his introduction Sibthorp wrote that he was extending his original work to cover every day of the year with a few verses attached to each, as a piece of butter to a slice of dry bread.

Death intervened just before he finished the work as it is 7 days short of completion! The main themes are evangelical although I did find one or two references to the Blessed Eucharist. Sykes considered that it was most likely to end up on the coffee tables of some Anglican rectories rather than in Catholic presbyteries.

The Tablet reviewed the book on October 4th 1879. It is an excellent example of how to damn a book with the faintest of praise.

> "We look upon this work as a monument of the interior piety and zeal of its excellent author rather than as a work of any great utility to the Catholic public. The best years of Mr Sibthorp's life were spent in the Evangelical school of the Church of England. In it he acquired a manner of thought and style of expression which he would seem never to have been able to lay aside. The result is that the book before us is written in what is almost a foreign language, certainly an unfamiliar dialect, to the Catholic reader. Such words as 'Jehovah' ,'Believer', 'Godliness', 'Saving Truth', 'Churchmanship' which frequently occur in Mr Sibthorp's meditations , are examples of what we mean. There is a preponderance too of the subjective element which is characteristic of the school to which the author so long belonged and will strike the Catholic mind as unusual. But another strongly marked feature of the book will be we think, the principle obstacle to its usefulness. Each meditation concludes with some verses. No indication is given of the sources from whence they are taken, and many of them are quite unfamiliar to us. But others are very familiar and are taken some of them from the 'Christian Year', and others from the 'Olney Hymn Book' while at least one is from the 'Lyra Apostolica', none of them as far as we know is from a Catholic source. There is probably nothing unorthodox in any of the poetry that Mr Sibthorp has embodied in his book, but there is a tone about it that jars with Catholic instincts and however beautiful the verses may be, few children of the Church would care to use them for purposes of devotion."

For the last two years of his life Sibthorp was more or less confined to his house getting weaker and weaker. He maintained his generosity to the poor and indeeed sold his entire collection of china to raise more funds for them. The sale catalgue, a copy of which can still be found in the

Downside Library would lead one to expect that it was kept on the ground floor. There are literally thousands of items, that any first floor would likely collapse under their weight !

One of the last events to affect him as he lay dying was the news that Newman had been made a Cardinal. Instead of rejoicing he was furious. He wrote to Fowler on March 7th 1879 "What a mistake Dr Newman has just made! Christ Jesus and none but He for me!"

When Fowler met him a few days later as death approached he returned to this theme."Tell the Bishop of Lincoln I think Dr.Newman has made a great mistake". At about the same time his old friend Dr. Bloxham received his final letter "I wish to express to you my entire and decided disapproval of Dr.Newman's last step; the Cardinal's hat; Oh, it is a very sad step, I don't mince the matter. You may let him know it. Whatever you do, do not be tempted to leave your present position."

What then caused this outburst ? It is certain that he did not really accept Papal infallibility at any time and that he had a particular loathing for ultramontanism. Fowler suggests possibly correctly that he saw that even Post Tridentine Rome had passed away and given place to "the Rome of Vatican Dogma...and as regards Churches and systems he feels that every prop and stay is falling away from him." My own view is that never at any time did he really understand what the Catholic Church truly was. He thought that Newman could keep the balance between the two bodies together, and that as soon as he accepted the Cardinal's Hat, he had abandoned all idea of this form of "via Media". Indecisive to the end, the last few days of his life almost offer an element of humour.

As a Catholic Priest he was of course the recipient of the Last rites of Holy Mother Church which he duly received a week or so before he died. But his favourite reading in his last few days was the Book of Common Prayer and in particular the funeral rites . At his death the Book of Common Prayer was by his side. When his will was opened it was discovered that a truly mixed funeral was envisaged. He was to be given a Requiem Mass at Nottingham Cathedral and then be taken off to the family grave at Lincoln where a clergyman of the Church of England was to conduct the final obsequies. So he was "facing both ways to the very end." The Bishop of Nottingham was broad minded enough to allow this order to be left intact and indeed preached the funeral oration. The Bishop was lavish in his praise of the departed.

"His faith in Christ was profound and sincere and he abhorred everything in that system of education which tries to do away with the revealed truth of Christianity...He had bright, happy and distinguishing virtues; and it was impossible to read the lines he had written (that is 'Daily Bread'), or to have listened to his conversation without feeling how he clung to the Divine Saviour. How edifying and beautiful his conversation always was !...His heart was also filled with charity to all men. Whoever heard him say a discourteous or unkind word to or about another ? They all knew what they owed to him in the completion of that church by its spire which was his gift, and they knew further his many works and boundless charity among the poor, how he gave to the Sisters, that they might give to feed the poor children; how he gave to the poor box, that the priests might be helped to give; how he assisted the hospital dispensary and other charities....His Divine Master would not fail him but would reward him with a noble, Divine and God like generosity.!"

The last words of the Bishop summed it all up:

> "They had a great example before them in his spirituality, his piety , and love for his Divine Lord, and they owed him a debt of gratitude for his charity and the benefits which had been derived from him,; for his alms and charity, which many of them had received and been grateful to him for."(23)

The remains were then taken to Lincoln cemetery where they were buried by the Chaplain to his Bedehouses. Only the members of his family were present, not even the Bedesmen.

Mr Gladstone evidentally approved of the strange circumstances of his burial. He told his biographer, Fowler:

> "The circumstance you have mentioned respecting his internment is most soothing , most touching. Doubtless his peace is now deep, and his light abundant. I can never think of him but as a simple rare, truly elect soul."

Fowler sent Gladstone his memoir and Gladstone, then Prime Minister wrote from 10, Downing St:

> "...During the crowded time which has since elapsed (since receiving it) I have read it through with interest delight and comfort, even greater than I had anticipated. I must confess that some part of the politics have pained and tried me, not in the slightest degree that part of them which affects myself, not the perplexing pheonomenon with which the last few years have made me so familiar, of an orthodoxy, piety, here even a strong spiritual insight in a most saintly elevation of character without any proportionate accuracy of perception in what seems to me some elementary questions of just and unjust. This is a drawback, but a drawback from a store so large , that the diminution seems scarcely perceptible, so pure, beautiful and holy, is the character and with such grace and natural thruthfulness does it present itself on the earthward side.
>
> I deeply mourn never to have enjoyed the opportunity I ever particularly longed for of working up into something like substance my shadowy acquaintance with him, whom we must term Father Sibthorp. I am very curious to see what impresion the book produces. The superficial facts of apparent change often repeated may repel many from the precious material which forms the substance. Two more sentences before I close.. you certainly had a difficult task to perform between loyalty to your friend and to your Church. As far as I may presume to judge you have performed it admirably. Further I am very desirous if there be any way of obtaining in a local bookshop or otherwise, a copy of the "Office of Holy Communion" which I see was twice published to be a possessor if it. There is surely force if not comprehensiveness or precision in his view of the Anglican Office, and I should gladly wish to know how he would have

Office, and I should gladly wish to know how he would have dealt with the case. It is curious to see how much his mind dwelt on the earthly side of the Church of England and this I should suppose was his only superstition, but I must stop in subscribing myself Rev and Dear Sir,

Faithfully Yours,
W.E.Gladstone. [24]

It speaks much for the character of Gladstone that in the midst of all the troubles of being a Prime Minister he could sit down and read the biography of a man he barely knew. What 20th Century Prime Minister while still in office would act likewise?

To sum up the enigma of Sibthorp is rather difficult. I think perhaps it is best to think of him as bird with legs on two twigs on the same branch of a tree which he thought of as the Church. Sometimes he rests more one twig than the other but ends up balanced equally on both. His idea of the Catholic Church was certainly Pre-Tridentine. One final quote from a letter he wrote a few years before his death may give the final clue.

"I am no Papist, I am a Catholic, an Old Catholic".

Notes and Sources.

The General outline of Sibthorp's life is taken from Fowler's biography. Both Sykes and Middleton use this as their base. Letters which have no notes attached to them are quoted from Fowler.

1) Quoted from the entry in the Dictionary of National Biography under Sibthorp, John.
2) R.D Middleton, *Magdalen Studies*, "Henry Best" page 185
3) "A Sermon on Phil.chap 1 verse 27, preached in St.John's Church, Hull, printed then in London (copy at Magdalen Library)
4) Sermon printed at Hull (copy at Magdalen Library)
5) "The Character of the Papacy as predicted by St Paul in 2

Thess...Chap ll verse 4. (London 1828)

6) Newman. *Letters and Diaries*. Vol 2 Dec 12th 1829. Newman to Rev...John Hill.
7) Fowler. p 44.
8) Bumpus - 2nd Series page 90.
9) Newman *Letters and Diaries* Vol 6. 30th November 1836
10) "History of St. James Ryde" page 5
11) "Sermon preached on the Feast of St. Mark the Evangelist AD 1841"
12) Pamphlet *Some Answer to the Enquiry why have you become a....Catholic* ? (London 1842)
13) Scheifen. *Nicholas Wiseman* (Shepherdstown USA) Page 125
14) Quoted by Fowler p.367.
15) Both letters quoted by Sykes page 54
16) *Memoirs of Kenelm Henry Digby* London 1919. page 90
17) Quoted by Middleton page 212
18) Middleton page 213
19) Sykes, page 58
20) Middleton page 219
21) Fowler page 173
22) Fowler page 255.
23) Fowler page 366
24) Found as copy in Sibthorp papers included in the Bloxham MS at Magdalen College Library.MS 492.

PART FOUR
Richard Simpson
Liberal Catholic

INTRODUCTION

The first three converts considered in this volume were all Protestant Clergymen who became Catholic Priests. Simpson was for a short while a clergyman but due to his marriage he was unable to move on to the Catholic Priesthood. He was very wealthy and as a layman had no need to earn his living. Thus he was able to spend all his time on research into his many interests. Far too many interests, for he became a dilettante. He wrote hundreds of articles on a wide variety of topics but few complete books and even these are compilations of magazine articles. His main line of interest as a Liberal Catholic was to attempt to reconcile Science and Faith and to bring Catholics out of what he considered a static frame of mind.

A biography already exists written by Fr Damian McElrath, and a dissertation by Geoffrey James on his philosophical and theological thought contains a fair amount of biographical information.His papers are to be found in three locations. The family papers including much background information are in Mitcham public Library in Surrey, the main bulk of letters and unpublished articles are in the Downside Library, while the correspondence with Lord Acton which has been printed of course, is at Fitzwilliam Library Cambridge.

In this essay I am more concerned with his religious faith than with his philosophical viewpoint though the two overlap to some extent. I also tried to use as much unpublished material as possible rather than merely requote from the *Rambler* articles or other works.

CHAPTER ONE.

From Birth to Conversion.

Richard Simpson was born in the Parish of Beddington, Surrey on the 16th September 1820 and baptised in the local church a few weeks later. He was the son of William

Simpson of Lichfield and the second of his four children by his wife Emily Cranmer.

The Simpson's were a distinguished family at Lichfield while the Cranmer family were even more prosperous. They claimed a relationship with the family of Archbishop Thomas Cranmer but the genealogy the family left in their papers (now at Mitcham Library) does not extend back to the 16th century. However in 1656 Robert Cranmer obtained the title to the Manor of Mitcham and at the same time the right of nomination to the Parish Church of Sts Peter and Paul.

All four of the Simpson children became Catholics. William, the eldest inherited the property, while Robert the youngest son became a Catholic Priest. Their daughter Emily became a nun at Taunton.The family archives at Mitcham Library preserve many of the letters of the Simpson children. Even at the age of 8, Richard was able to write in an adult hand, but was then obliged by his school masters or by his parents to write in cursive script. Only after he arrived at Merchant Taylor's school does he revert to an adult hand.Initially he attended a private boarding school run by the Rev. Charles Delafosse at Richmond, Surrey. Later he moved to a small private boarding school run by James Tobias Cook at Whittlesea near Peterborough. His letters home show an interest in Church architecture and sketching.

He entered Merchant Taylor's School, then situated on the site of the present Cannon St. Station in 1831. The headmaster James Bellamy, was anxious to reform the curriculum just at the time Simpson was a student there. So in addition to the usual classics he was able to study Mathematics and Geography. Richard was evidently well thought of and became a Monitor. In later life though he did not think much of the education provided and complained about the paucity of scholarship holders at Oxford who had been at Merchant Taylor's. He wrote to a friend "What else can you expect from a man like Bellamy who substitutes twaddle for taste and prejudice for judgement?" Although he himself topped the list for a scholarship to Oxford he was passed over in favour of the third on the list, a Mr McKie. Richard entered Oriel in 1839 at the same time as R.W. Church took up the post of tutor there.

At the time of his entry as with the other colleges, Oriel continued to control completely the required lectures for its students. However just at the time of Simpson's arrival, Oriel began to lose its pre-eminence amongst the Oxford colleges in favour of Balliol. Up to the mid thirties Oriel had been dominated by its great Fellows, John Henry Newman, Thomas Arnold, John Keble and Richard Whately. The decline of Oriel set in when the new provost Edward Hawkins, dismissed Newman, Hurrell Froude, and Robert Wilberforce as college Tutors and substituted second class replacements. He was totally opposed to the Tractarian movement and questioned all his students personally, erasing them from the college books if ever they converted to Rome.While at Oxford Simpson became very inerested in the relationship between Geology and Genesis. The prominent Geologist, Charles Lyell had just published his "Principles of Geology". The basic premise was that existing forces in the Universe given time enough would account for the observable state of the earth. For Lyell, all change was uniform..there would be little room for the direct intervention of God, so the story of the Flood would be a myth. Lyell prepared the way for Darwin and the theological problems involved in his theories would later be taken up by St George Mivart.

Meanwhile Simpson's notebooks indicate a deep interest in Mosaic Cosmogony. He made a special study of the issues involved and began to formulate an ethic that would guide his whole career as a writer. First the right of the scientist to pursue his subject, unimpeded by outmoded theological prohibitions; and the need for the theologian to to interpret revelation in the context of contemporary scientific research and not by outdated scientific theory.

The other main influence on Simpson at the University was of course the Tractarian movement. Two characteristics particularly attracted him, the orientation towards personal piety and the importance of the Sacramental principle, in particular the Eucharist. He was also impressed by the importance of rites and ceremonies and much influenced by Keble and his work *Christian Year* first published in 1827. Indeed Keble was a greater influence than Newman at this time on Simpson. The only time he ever met Newman was a trivial matter over which he needed to see Newman as college Bursar. At that time though Simpson was accepting Newman's views about Faith and Reason. For Newman the safeguard of the faith was the state of holiness, dutifulness and love ; and the intellect and logic were insufficient as safeguards [1]. After meeting Lord Acton Simpson would come to restrict this principle.

Simpson's attraction to the Tractarians became known to his parents and his tutors. His parents had already been dismayed to be see their eldest son William displaying the same sympathies at Trinity College, Cambridge. He became a Catholic in 1843 while Robert became a Catholic in 1845 after studying at St. John's College, Oxford.

When he entered Oxford Richard already had in mind the Anglican ministry. It was not difficult for an undergraduate to take orders. All that was necessary was to attend the lectures on the 39 articles and compose a number of sermons. Some of these sermons are still to be found amongst his papers. Much later on Simpson was asked to comment on the possibility of admitting Catholic students to Oxford and he wrote in 1864:

> "Not the Universities, but the Colleges have been and are Protestant Seminaries. When I was at Oxford the theological faculty of the University was a nullity. Dr. Hampden, Regius Professor of Divinity was under a cloud. His lectures consisted chiefly of lists of books he recommended us to read and during his lectures most of us were reading books he did NOT recommend. Dr.Faucett, the Lady Margaret Professor of Divinity had

just been endowed like Bottom with an Asses head through a pamphlet of Mr Newman and a contemptupous article in the *British Critic* comparing him to a fat poodle dog which accurately represented the feelings of the majority of undergraduates towards him. The great influence was outside the University in Mr Newman's Parish Church." [2]

The Downside papers preserve a very early prepared sermon dating from December 1841. He took as his theme Psalm 99 verse 8. "Thou answerest them O Lord Our God. Thou wast a God who forgave them, tho thou tookest vengeance of their inventions."

Simpson argues that both in the old Testament and the early Church God both chastises people and forgives them their sins. He forgives them *because* he chastises them. "Whenever love began to wan cold, and worldliness began to eat as a canker into the Church, so surely did He send a persecution among them - He chastises them but he heard them too." The case was rather different today. The Church of England is in a bad way. "The sun and moon are darkened, the stars refuse their light - we probe about in the noonday and became as blind men. Of old when a sin was committed, summary vengenace was inflicted and men saw it and feared and repented, now the Church goes on and all things seem to go on as before - God puts not forth his hand to punish."

This reflection leads Simpson to conclude by looking at the ways in which our duty lies if God is not in fact punishing us. These final reflections show Tractarian influence at work.

"1. As He now affords less evidence of His presence in the Church there is a greater scope for faith afforded, greater faith to see our way through the darkness.

2. As he has ceased to punish us for our sins, it is left that we should punish ourselves if He brings not persecution upon us. It is that we ourselves should supply its place with fasting and hardship, that we should impose on ourselves those penances which in the their youth, the Church imposed on the erring sons.

3. As he has hidden Himself, that we should watch and pray more and more earnestly.

4. Humility and self abasement for the sins which have caused Him to withdraw.

5. increased Love, for its was our lukewarness that cast us out of his mouth.

6. Increased zeal for his name that we bear not so patiently the blasphemy of the multitude. If we perform all these duties, no doubt he will return to us. If he comes with a nod, let us kiss the nod, and He will give us Heaven for earth. If he returns in peace, blessed be His Holy Name."

Simpson graduated with 2nd Class in Humanities at the end of the Michaelmas Term in 1842. He was given permission to stand for an Oriel Fellowship the fellowing year but did not obtain one by the competition of 1843. In that year he was ordained deacon on the 24th Septmber and licensed to assist in the Church and Chapel of Dratton and Dilton in the County of Wiltshire. He was ordained priest at Salisbury Cathedral on Sunday 22nd Septmber 1844 and presented by his parents to the Parish of Mitcham. Less than two years later he would renounce his allegiance to the Church of England to join the Catholic Church.

There are examples of Simpson's sermons both at Downside and in the Mitcham Library collections and they show strong Tractarian influence.There are eloquent words on ceremonial, architecture, painting, and sculpture as applied to Christian Art. He often dwelt as did Keble on the themes of symbolism and sacrament. He had no room for justification by faith alone or personal arbitrary interpretation of Holy Scripture.

What the poor parishioners thought of his sermons is not recorded.It was not by any means a wealthy parish. There were a goodly number of leading families but also a great number of "the labouring Classes" most of them illiterate. Indeed Simpson wrote just before taking up his post,

"I shall not talk at Mitcham because there is no one to talk to but I hope I shall do something strong. I shall

> make up my mind to be on bad terms with the respectable if they will not keep on good terms with me I am persuaded that the poor are the clergyman's chief care and I am sure that if I can begin well among them I shall eventually get on well enough among all".

One person he was certainly NOT on good terms with was his Bishop none other than Bishop Sumner of Winchester in whose diocese Mitcham then was. Wilfred Ward writes "disputes with his Bishop had become such a necessary part of his daily life that he could no more do without them than some men can dispense with a daily constitutional." Exactly what the problems were I was not able to discover but Simpson did not remain long at Mitcham.

In 1846 Simpson decided to become a Catholic. He wrote a letter to a friend called Ashworth stating he no longer believed the 39 articles and was more at home with Catholic Priests than with Anglican Clergymen. Before he left the Parish he made a farewell speech to his parishioners at Mitcham. This is an apology to his flock for deserting them so soon after arriving. Much of the sermon is devoted to the teaching on the Blessed Eucharist. Here are a few extracts which show the line of his thought.

> "When Christ gave the apostles their commission, He breathed on them and said, 'Receive ye the Holy Ghost, so he commanded them to baptise with water for the redemption of sin, and to give His Body and Blood under the forms of bread and wine. Such was the way in which the founder of our religion used outward things to convey to us inward gifts. Is it credible then that this use is contrary to the spirit of religion ? Is it credible that He adopted the custom merely to satisfy the Jews but that He did not intend it to continue in His Church ? Could the Wisdom of God be so shortsighted as to establish His Fabric on a foundation that was about to be destroyed ? Yet such must be the belief of those that contend that our religion has nothing to do with outward forms. Nay more, the Atonement is not safe with them. That doctrine is that we are redeemed by the actual and true death of Christ

upon the Cross. That our souls are cleansed by the loss of Blood which ame forth from His wounds. How is not this a spiritual blessing effected by external and visible means? The Blood of Chist is no mere shadow, no dream, no unreal mystical idea but the true substantial Blood as real as the blood of our bodies

How can a little Blood shed eighteen centuries ago on a hill near Jerusalem, redeem your soul ? God has annexed spiritual blessings to material forms, as He has joined the Godhead to the Manhood, or the soul to the Body. You cannot cast away the doctrine of sacraments and keep the doctrine of the atonement. They must stand or fall together."

He goes on to speak about the Sacrifice of Christ and the Mass.

"The sacrifice of the death of Christ was once offered and now He dieth no more and there is no other sacrifice. Now in the Eucharist it is not pretended that Christ is put to death or His Body broken or His Blood poured out. The outward symbols, the shapes of bread and wine are broken and poured out, in order to 'show forth' or RE-PRESENT 'His death till he comes' but he is not mangled or slain. His Body is spiritual and impassible. As when He spoke to Nicodemus he was wholly on earth, so in the Eucharist He is wholly present in each form and when the form is broken He is still whole and undivided. He is perfectly present in every particle of the consecrated elements by virtue of the spirituality of His Body, some of the effects of which I have before described

..Such being my belief with regard to the Eucharist, I cannot remain in a position which supposes my assent to the Articles of the English Church. I do not believe that the clergy of the Anglican Church can administer a valid Eucharist but if they can, such consequences ensue as oblige me to abstain from their communion. I can no longer be at peace where Priest and people receive without faith, not discerning the Lord's Body, where crumbs of the Bread of Life are dropped about, the consecrated Wine smeared over the lips of the communicants and wiped off with their handkerchiefs, and no care taken that no drops are left in the Chalice when what remains of the Consecrated Bread is consumed "[3]

Simpson himself wrote in his diary for 1846 "On the Octave of the Feast of Sts Peter and Paul I resigned my living and on the feast of St Peter's Chains, August lst, Mary and I were received into the Catholic Church and made our lst Communion the day after. On Sunday August 9th we made our 2nd Holy Communion and were aftwerwards in consequence of our consanguinity, by dispensation of Bishop Griffiths remarried by Fr. Brownbill."

These points require a little explanation. Fr. Brownbill was a Jesuit Priest based in London. It was during his time at Mitcham that he married his second cousin, Mary Cranmer. Such a marriage in the Catholic Church needs a dispensation for its validity and that is why they went through the re-marriage. Today that is known as the process of convalidation which however is normally applied when one or both the parties are Catholic but failed to marry in the Catholic Church in the first instance. In the case of consanguinity (close relationship by blood) the Church regards the impediment as affecting the marriages of ALL BAPTISED Christians of whatever faith. In the normal way, the marriage of two baptised Christians IS considered as valid and there is no need of a further ceremony.

We know very little about Mary. They became Catholics together but there were no children of the marriage. Indeed in practical terms we know very little of Simpson's day to day life afterwards. What little we glean comes from the public events in which he was involved and little glimpses from his letters. The only diaries which survive are for the journey to Rome in 1846 and 1847 and for the last full year of his life 1875. We do know that he was comfortably well off. A Settlement from the family meant he could live without having to work for a living. In 1862 he had an income of £700.00 from investmentsand was able to buy a share the *Rambler* with which he is so closely associated. From 1848 they lived on Clapham Common in Victoria

Terrace quite close to the Church of St. Mary's where Coffin was to live for most of his life. The Simpson's were regular worshippers at this Church.

CHAPTER TWO
Journey to Rome, and the influence of Lord Acton

The Simpson's left for a years leisurely visit to Rome while he decided what his future might be. The journey is described in his diary or journal (Notebook 43 in the Downside Simpson Papers). Here I give some excerpts which illustrate well the way Simpson was already thinking. The following excerpts have been printed in the Downside Review for October 1945 .

Although Simpson was not present he describes the sermons preached by Newman for the funeral of a Miss Bryan, the niece of the Earl of Shrewsbury. The sermon did not go down well because in the sermon he started making remarks about Protestants who were present at the ceremony. Nor was the sermon appreciated by Old Catholics who lived in Rome. Simpson then has this to say about the Old Catholics:

> "The Old Catholics had cerainly become listless and sleepy; they did not convert us. The movement arose from among ourselves,the Old Catholics rather retarded it than assisted it. The consequence is that there is now an inundation of men versed in controversy and writing, very much into their hands, and the Old Catholics find themselves in the background. Besides this, many of the Old Catholics think that those who by their private judgement and search have found for themselves the truth, will have such a habit of searching and judging that they will not be long contented with submission to authority."

The Roman auhtorities themselves are too self contented...

> "Such is very much the case with (Cardinal) Perrone and the theological lecturers in Rome. They have had no one to dispute with them, so they have got into the way of smoothing over all difficulties, to refer every

omission every fault, to the 'disciplina arcani' and to their own entire satisfaction to demolish every Protestant objection whether a priori or historical, which of course they too care to state in their own terms and to make egregiously ridiculous. This is all very well for the city of Rome and for Italy where no controversy ever comes. But for England , Germany and France, it will never do. The mouths of Protestants can never be stopped by the old humdrum answers; the experience of 300 years one would think is enough to prove that."

There were many things that upset Simpson in Rome. The kind of visitors there for one:

"Moreover during the season it is one of the most dissipated places in the world. Not I mean for vice, for nothing of that is seen, no immodesty, no drunkeness, but a for continual whirl of giddy parties etc etc. These are the great attractions which draw the English to Rome."

Although he thought the Roman Clergy were in general quite exemplary, he came across rather a different type of cleric.

"This is the place to which all priests who have quarrelled with their Bishop come for redress, all who are suspended come to prosecute their appeals. Such men as these will say Masses , bow low to the Madonnas, frequent the sanctuaries, till they can find themselves in a Chaplaincy or other snug place when they can throw off the mask and shew again their real characters. Moreover, the suspended and scandalous Priests are usually the very ones who get themselves introduced into Protestant families as tutors to their children, when of course they represent the whole clergy as sunk into the abominable viciousness the viciousness of their lives furnishes the Protestant with an example from which he is but too ready to judge the whole Catholic Priesthood." (4)

While in Rome he attended the Holy Father's Mass more than once and met Newman once or twice including breakfasting with him at the English College.

After he returned to England he began to make a name

for himself as a lecturer. This started after he took on one Dr Cummings who attacked the presence of the Redemptorists at Clapham in 1848. Simpson rushed to their aid in defending the Catholic doctrine of invoking the saints in prayer. At Clapham too he met with Isaac Hecker who as a Redemptorist was studying for the priesthood with a view to working in America. He left the order in 1858 to find the Paulist order as he felt that a new order was necessary to promote new ideas and new techniques for spreading the faith and converting America to Rome.

Simpson maintained friendship with Hecker who shared his ideals and their correspondance is to be found in the Downside papers.

Also at Clapham Simpson held meetings with other converts including Frederick Capes, brother of the founder of the *Rambler* and Peter le Page Renouf who would take an active role in the Liberal Catholic Movement.

Simpson though was drifting at this time. He was moaning again about the lack of use made by the hierarchy of the converts. He wrote to Hecker:

> "About 400 Parsons converted (about 100 or 150 of whom are priests) all anxious to do what they can and yet no Bishop with 'vous' sufficent to use them as catechists, or lecturers or anything else; the clergy deprecating their meddling,..and thinking it more intolerable to have to suffer the impertinence of a few bumptious converts than to see around them a mass of heathenism on which they feel themselves quite powerless to make any impression." [5]

The *Rambler* magazine was to prove the main outlet for Simpson's liberal ideas. It is not the intention here to go over the controversy caused by the *Rambler* articles but rather to examine them in the light of modern day thinking. The thought behind the movement is essentially the reconciliation of science with the faith, a need which exists in every age as more and more discoveries are made. Looking back now on the difficulties faced by the early liberal Catholics we are entitled to say that the effective suppression of the movement in 1864 led to a hardening of attitudes and prepared the ground for the modernism of the next generation. Not that the Liberal Catholics would have become modernists necessarily. Acton, their leader, played no part deliberately in the early stages of modernism. Mivart though as the next essay will show, supported the liberal Catholics and then accepted many of the modernists views. But he was in no way theologically trained while both Acton and Simpson were. They both knew where to draw the line on questions of dogma. Mivart did not and ended up excommunicated.

This is however looking ahead. Simpson started writing for the *Rambler* in 1850 but Acton did not become involved until at least 1858 and trouble had already started by the time he came on the scene.

The first articles to suggest trouble in store appeared in the autumn months of 1850. They dealt with the relationship between Genesis and Geology. Here the problem was not so much that Simpson denied the Mosaic account of creation for in fact he accepted it broadly, but that he stated in the interpretation of Scripture the Church had limited rights..What he meant was that one kind of truth (biblical) cannot contradict another type of truth (scientific). At that stage however, even this proposition seemed to some to be proximate to heresy. As always in his *Rambler* articles he argued that a freedom of debate and a fresh theological approach where necessary.

In 1852 he had stated about Galileo that the Church could however sometimes limit the pursuit of knowledge if the weak might be scandalised by the truth. By 1856 such a limitation was far from his mind. There was no question about it. Truth cannot be "offensive to pious ears".

The first really serious problem though came in 1856 when Simpson published a set of articles on Original Sin. These led Cardinal Wiseman to set up a commission to investigate the problems involved in the articles to search out for possible heresy.[6]

Now before looking at the ideas put forward, it is necessary to point out that he did not deny the propagation of original sin as arising from the fall of Adam. Nowhere is it suggested that original sin is a kind of accumulation of the worlds sins or other modern theories which cause so much of a problem at the end of the 20th century. The points that Simpson makes are of quite a technical order involving the natural and supernatural end of man's existence on earth. The attack on the articles came first of all from the commission set up to look into the articles after they were written and then much later by Bishop Ullathorne in his comprehensive attack on most of the *Rambler*'s articles. This was published as a whole in "A Second Letter to the Clergy of the Diocese of Birmingham on Certain Methods of the Rambler and the Home and Foreign Review." The letter is dated January 26th 1863.

First of all the specific points which the commission were asked to look into were that the articles denied the following truths. 1) That God wills all to be saved, so he ordained all to a supernatural end. 2) God gives to all sufficient grace to (attain) a supernatural end. 3) Christ died for All.

Coffin was one of the three commission members. Another was Dr. Todd, a distinguished theologian and a convert himself who commented on those points. He wrote back to Coffin on 26th Feb 1856 a long detailed account of his findings. Here is a little from the reply:

> "I object first of all to the new terminology adopted by this writer when treating of very difficult and intricate questions of theology - I think his terminology is untheological, inaccurate and confused. For instance where is his authority for dividing sin into 'degradation' and 'lapse', and what does he mean by these terms? He tells us that degradation is passive when a rational agent without his own act, finds himself placed in a lower grade than his nature was originally intended to fill. If this is meant to apply to original sin, it might do as an inadequate illustration, but it fails as a theological

definition. The consequence of Original Sin is not mainly degradation but a real FALL, (Lapsus). The fall of human nature is in consequence of the voluntary sin of the same human nature. The term 'lapse' (ie as used by Simpson) is confused because strictly it includes Original Sin and I suppose all that the writer means by it would be better expressed by the common term 'actual sin'."

Later at the end of the letter he sums up:

"Upon the whole my criticism upon this paper as well as upon the article in the *Rambler* would be that the writer has not analysed with sufficient care the thoughts and ideas on this subject that are in his own mind, and that he has incurred his difficulties in consequence of his not being familiar with (or at least not employing) the ordinary but in these matters, very necessary, scientific language."

This letter was sent by Todd to Coffin and with it was a sheet of writing in Latin by Simpson as if in answer to some of the points being made against him. He makes some distinctions as follows

(Translation) "God wishes infants to be saved and therefore orders them to a supernatural end.

Nonetheless he has prepared a limbo of children where lacking a supernatural end, they enjoy a natural end. Here too adults who without any fault of their own are unaware of a supernatural end will be found according to the great theologian St Gregory Nazianzen. Also Dante writes thus of the limbo of the Fathers, the same limbo from which Christ took the souls of the Holy Patriarchs. ' Le turbe ch'eran molte e grandi, D'infanti, e di femmine e di viri' So what Dante believed, why should I not believe ? 2) God gives sufficient grace to all towards their end, I agree, but to a supernatural end I deny unless it is to be found in ecclesiastical formulae." (The remainder of this quote is scratched out).

The point made here is quite interesting in that the traditional belief in the state of Limbo has been attacked more recently for precisely the same reason. That it assumes that a large number of people are indeed destined to a purely natural end, the state of limbo, where they neither enjoy the beatific vision, nor are they in the depths of hellfire. On this issue today many would say that the fate of the unbaptised may be covered by the Salvific will of God and some extension of baptism of desire. It is and always will be a very difficult point. In the light of the theological thinking of the time what Simpson says could not be condemned as downright heretical.[6]

Now in 1856 these were the main points raised against the articles but Ullathorne in his letter to the clergy found several more points of disagreement. However the difficulties seem to lie in Simpson's refusal to use the word "Propagation" and refer instead to "inheriting" when dealing of the way in which we have original sin at our births. Here then are the key passages. The first one is from the *Rambler* July 1855 page 27.

> "But though man was degraded, his nature continued intact; there still remained in him the faculty by which he could enjoy God; what he wanted was the supernatural assistance to enable him to attain to the object of this faculty. Man therefore was left in an abnormal condition; created for one purpose and applied to another; and at the same time incapable of receiving perfect satisfaction for the whole of his faculties by the complete attainment of this substituted end. This degradation constitutes the guilt of original sin; and it is only in this sense that guilt can be inherited.
>
> This degradation is the natural inheritance of every child of Adam, because the degraded is the natural state; the original was a supernatural state.
>
> We inherit original sin, because we inherit nature, and only nature by natural propagation."

While one may perhaps allow a Catholic interpretation of this statement, a few lines later he does come out with some very strange ideas. (on page 35 of the same issue)

> "The law of the propagation of anything that can be called sin must be sought not in nature, but in the will of

God and in His attributes of love mercy, purity and justice.The act by which He causes original sin to be inherited cannot be the result of mere vengeance or of justice untempered by mercy. We must rather seek its reason in the principle so much insisted on by St Paul, that sin is not imputed where the law is not; that those who have not heard Christ's words nor seen his works, but are blind, have not sin. God therefore concluded in unbelief that he might have mercy upon all. He degraded man to a lower order where the supernatural law bound him not that he might not be liable to the extreme punishment of those who transgress it. We are therefore born in sin because it is good for us".

Indeed a very strange idea which Ullathorne was quick to seize upon. Later Simpson would defend himself by saying that this was implied in the teaching of Cardinal Perrone, a standard theologian of the Roman School of the time. Quoting Perrone:

"Original sin in us means the want of the grace and gifts which Adam lost by sin, and the privation of them if we regard the personal fault of Adam. Hence we are neither made worse nor do we incur any positive corruption of nature except in relation to what this first condition required. Hence original sin neither brought upon us a necessity of sinning, nor are innocent persons punished for others sins,nor are other sins imputed to us."

This quote is to be found from a pamphlet written by Simpson entitled *Bishop Ullathorne and the Rambler-Reply to Cricicisms.* The pamphlet was produced in 1862 and with a postcript added in 1863.

Before leaving this topic entirely, it is interesting to see that in 1856 Simpson was trying to give a Catholic interpretation to the theory of evolution., a point which Mivart would develop later.

"Why did God place man on earth when He knew that he would fall? Is it not more rational to suppose that he was introduced into the animal world which up to the time of his creation had through myriads of ages been gradually progressing from the lowest to the highest types of animal life - not with a sudden jerk, not with such an immeasurable interval, as is implied in the sudden introduction of the angel-like Adam and Eve, but with a slight step, and advance on the monkey little greater than that of the ape beyond the genus next below it? It would be more in accordance with analogy that man should come in as a link in a series, as natural science teaches, than as a magnificent solecism, a grand exception, utterly unlike anything else in nature. Man in this view has only progressed, he has never fallen; he began a naked savage in the woods, little removed from the ourang-outang; by his superior cerebral organisation he has gradually advanced to what he is. According to the Christian view he was exceptionally introduced into a world that for ages had been governed by the most uniform laws, introduced as an angel, wise and good, only to become almost immediately more devil than angel, foolish, weak and criminal.

Now so far as man is only animal there is no reason for denying the progress here asserted. In the natural point of view, Adam is simply the highest link in the animal series; he was not a civilised man; he had no notion of mechanics, or cookery, or music or painting or sculpture; he only knew what God revealed to him. There is no reason for denying that natural acquirements as distinguished from supernatural, were at their minimum in Adam, and have made enormous progress since his time."

and later,

"as rational being, as a being made for the supernatural, he was not less gradually to discover in the course of generations, the existence and the destiny of his soul. His creation was a miracle. He had the supernatural gift to shew him what his nature was intended for; then he was allowed to LAPSE into the mere animal condition in order that it might redound to the glory of God of such stones to raise up successors to the fallen cherubim. If Adam had never posssessed the gift, man introduced as an animal would have remained so; he would have resigned himself contentedly to his lot, would have used his reason for the sole end of fortifying and assisting his animal instincts. ..It would not have struck him that his miseries and mortality imported degradation any more than natural sufferings of any other animals implied they had fallen from a higher state

It was only the tradition of a better state (ie primitive revelation) that made man perceive the evils of the present and set himself to amend them."

Ullathorne took this to mean that Adam was but a savage brute unconcious of a soul and led on only by concupiscence.He was not then an intellectual creature except by grace and that only for a transitory moment.

In 1856 the matters were settled amicably and Simpson agreed not to pursue the matter of original sin. He turned his attention at that point to recusant history and by this means became a reputable scholar both in recusancy and later in Shakesperian studies. However Simpson's difficulties continued and one has to ask what prompted him to take such controverial positions not only on original sin, but on other issues that were to come up. Fr. McElrath quotes from a letter of Canon Maguire of the Westminster Chapter which he says puts his finger on this issue. Simpson's mistake is to hold "So long as a proposition is not against faith you are free to assert it. If a theory is tenable and 'tenable' you consider as synonymous with 'possibly true', you can claim a right to publish it."

Certainly this was Simpson's attitude and he tended to put forward his views in a very aggressive manner. But except for the final issue of Papal Infallibility he either withdrew statements which were censureable or was proven right on many issues later on.

To conclude this section it is interesting to notice this aggressive style in an unpublished review of Fr.Faber's work *The Spirit of St. Philip Neri.* This exists as a manuscript in the Downside Library.

"Though a young priest, flushed with success and feeling that he is working for the glory of God, and that God is blessing his labours, ought to be borne with patiently in his little eccentricities, it sometimes becomes the duty of those who can watch his motions without passion or prejudice to say a few words when he appears to be running into error or extreme opinions - we are alluding now to Father Faber of the London Oratory and to his late work *The Spirit and Genius of St Philip Neri* That his tendency to reactionary extremes is shewn by his treatment of Gothic architecture. When he was a brother of the Will of God at St. Wilfred's he exalted that art into an essential END of Christianity- when he saw his error he ran into a contrary extreme and now as an Oratorian, he will not even use it as a MEANS of Worship. Rather he would do away with it altogether - This tendency of his. though it excuses him personally for many strange vagaries, is rather dangerous and ought to be most strictly watched over.

With that preface we will state what are our views with regard to his late work - it appears to us that Fr. Faber taking it for granted that it is the office of the Church to absorb all philosophies and modes of thought which have any 'go' in them, and exercise power and influence over the world - as Clement of Alexandria, Origen, and others platonised when the world was Platonic, and St.Thomas and the schoolmen Aristotelised when Aristotle was the regnant mode of thought - so in these latter times when thought is transcendental - when men who think at all, think in the language of Carlyle, Fournier and Emerson, it must be the vocation of some Catholics to transplant the new fashion into the Church and make the spouse of Christ accomodate her divine lips to the hard, disjointed, illogical, inconsequent diction of a disciple of Emerson!And who can have this vocation if not the brilliant passionate impetuous Faber!"

and later on in the review he is even more cutting:

"Faber like Emerson trusts to his instincts and feelings, he is in a truer sense than he would like to own, a Catholic Methodist - he is not inspired but he takes his passion and his feelings for inspirations, and so he scrawls them down and blurts them out."

One might well comment that Simpson himself did just that!

CHAPTER 3
Simpson and Acton Working Together 1858-1865

In 1858 John Dalberg Acton returned to England. Acton was the son of Sir Ferdinand Acton who inherited the Acton family estates at Aldenham. His mother Marie Louise Pelline was daughter of the Duke of Dalberg and through her Acton inherited their estates at Herrnsheim near Worms. Following the death of his father, his mother came to England and in 1840 married Lord Leveson, later Earl Granville.

Young John was sent for a short time to Oscott but was soon sent back to Germany to study under Ignaz von Dollinger, the priest historian. He joined Dollinger in his extensive travels and quickly impressed his tutor by his retentive memory and search for knowledge of all types. By the time he returned to England aged only 24 his intellectual development far exceeded that of any of his contemporaries in England. While in Germany he had met up with the German theological school and this led him to be a natural leader of the English Liberal Catholics, blending together the insights of German thought with the incisive mind of Simpson and his companions at the Rambler.

Needing a platform to communicate his ideas to his co-religionists he quickly became co-owner of the Rambler and acted as assistant editor to Simpson. Simpson saw at once that Acton had superior erudition and relied on Acton for ideas in his own articles.Their business relationship soon blossomed into a lasting friendship and their correspondence has been printed in three volumes [7].

The first phase of collaboration in the *Rambler* lasted until February 1859 when Simpson was asked to stand down as editor. The English Bishops had been very annoyed by certain articles attacking their policy on Catholic Education. As early as 1856 Dr J.G Wenham had attacked the Hierarchy's policy in running the Catholic Poor Schools and outlining their deficencies . Wenham himself was a distinguished Oxford convert, friendly with Newman and appointed as the director of Catholic Education in the Diocese of Southwark. He was at least slightly inclined to liberal Views and later clashed with Cardinal Manning over a catechism. He helped Simpson in 1872 when it seems that the local clergy at Clapham were inclined to refuse the Sacraments to Simpson who was seriously ill at the time.

An article apppeared in the February 1859 by Mr Scott Nasmyth Stokes in answer to complaints raised against the Rambler in the *Tablet*. The particular issue which had been rumbling on for some time was the degree of government interference which could be tolerated in the running of Catholic Schools in order to obtain a decent grant.

It seems that the Hierarchy were now refusing to co-operate with a Royal Commission to enquire into Education, on the grounds that none of the Commissioners were Catholic and the Bishops would not tolerate non-Catholic Commissioners prowling around Catholic Schools. Matters were not helped by the fact the negotiations with the government were supposed to be conducted by the Poor Schools Committee set up in 1847 but this body was being by-passed. Furthermore at the time the *Rambler* article appeared, nothing official had been pronounced.

This did not halt the ire of the Bishops who demanded that Simpson be removed as editor. The net result was the suspension of the magazine until a new Editor was appointed. This was to be Newman.

In the July issue for 1859 he wrote what was to prove the most famous article the *Rambler* ever printed. "On consulting the Faithful in matters of Doctrine "

There is little point in going over the controvesy which arose but their Lordships in England could not have been well pleased with the final lines of the article (page 230) which read

> "I think certainly that the Ecclesia Docens is more happy when she has such enthusiastic partisans about her as are here represented, than when she cuts off the faithful from the study of her divine doctrines and the sympathy of her divine contemplations, and requires from them a FIDES IMPLICITA in her word, which in the educated classes will terminate in indifference, and in the poorer superstition."

Such sentiments of course were exactly those of Simpson . Talbot expressed the opposite with his remarks about the role of the educated laity being limited to hunting and shooting, to which might be added praying and paying!

Simpson held Newman in high regard even though his own views were way ahead of the learned Oratorian. In an unpublished MSS History at Downside he gives this appreciation:

> "It was only after 1850 tht Dr Newman stood forth as a Catholic teacher. He is in England at least, the apostle and prophet of development because he has realised it both as a psychological and as an historical fact. He has led the doctrine as well as taught it..
>
> His Catholic Faith is intellectually only the development of the principles which he preached before the University of Oxford. To his mind, development is not so much the logical as the physiological growth of an idea. Not only the reason but all the powers of the soul work together to make the result. It is the unconscious, gradual and spontaneous growth of ideas habitual to the mind. Its processes are secret and unnoticed. Doctrinal development is latent in the spirit and temper of christians, and in popular prejudices. It grows in and out of the mass of human speculation, extravagance and error from which it is only gradually extricated and distinguished either by certain tests or in the case of the Church, by an external determinative authority as well. This theory while it triumphantly fills up the otherwise inadequate historical proof of certain dogmas, being held 'semper et ubique et ab omnibus' (always, everywhere and by everyone), also determines the sphere in which alone the decisions of ecclesiastical authority can be given.

Its affirmative decision must be first of all, development or growth of priorities as opposed to manufactured opinions, arbitrary assumptions, and ephemeral ideas created by leading articles as extemporaneous answers to accidental objections. Secondly, they must be developments which have always satisfied the tests by which development is distinguished from corruption; that is they must historically be true. As the intellectual decisions of the Church must necessarily be conformable to the prior and more general law of reason, So moral decisions must be conformable to the older and more intimate authority, the necessary laws of conscience. So too, historical decisions that certain doctrines were or were not in substance revealed to the apostles and have or have not been held 'semper, ubique, et ob omnibus' ever since, must conform to the primary and fundamental laws of historical evidence and method.

These considerations can account for two of the most prominent features of Dr. Newman's practical philosophy. Development requires the free action of the developing body. Now, in Christianity, the developing body is the whole Church, not clergy only, but laity ; and the faith which is developed is a thing which as Pope Nicholas first says ' is universal, common to all, pertaining not just to clergy but also to the laity.' For this reason he says, laymen had thin representations in synods where faith was discussed. Development of the faith implies therefore the education of the laity as an integral part of the developing body."

Although the reader may well agree with the sentiments here expressed, he or she may wonder why he used such long sentences. Indeed the length of the sentences and the many ideas contained in them may have contributed to the overall lack of understanding shown by the hierarchy for his thinking.

Simpson had been asked to step down as editor in 1859 as a direct result of two articles. One by Acton suggested that St Augustine must be regarded as the father of Jansenism and the other article was that by Scott Nasmyth Stokes on education which has been referred to already.

Although then Simpson was responsible for neither article he was blamed by the Bishops for the general tone of the magazine and for his own articles on Original Sin. Thus when Newman resigned after only two issues another editor had to be sought. This was Thomas Wetherell, himself an Oxford Convert and a civil servant at the War Office. When the Rambler was relaunched as the *Home and Foreign.* he objected because Simpson reamined a co-proprietor. He considered that any association of Simpson with the Review would create difficulties for the newly formed magazine. Simpson felt he was being edged out of the *Home and Foreign* and a compromise was eventually reached whereby the editorial policy was decided by a five man board including Acton Simpson and Wetherell.

These back room squabbles did not in any way diminish Simpson's literary activity for the new journal. The *Home and Foreign* was regarded very highly for the standard of its articles, many of them by Simpson personally. It was now that he started writing the life of Edmund Campion which appeared in instalments over the years. Later he published the complete life as a single volume. The last few chapters which did not appear in the magazine were added for the publication.This work still stands as an example to all future biographers of the English Martyrs for the close attention given to original source material in archives and state collections.

Even this work did not escape criticism from the hierarchy. Simpson claims that the action of the Holy Father in excommunicating Queen Elizabeth in 1570 hardened public opinion against Catholics, led to the large number of martyrdom's and caused the end of Catholicism as an active force in this country. Many historians today would agree with this line of reasoning but coming at a time when ANY criticism of the Holy Father was considered as tantamount to disobedience, it did not go down too well. At the same time reviews and articles were appearing which attacked the management of the Papal states. Although Simpson and Acton were not opposed to the idea of having such bodies as Papal States in order to guarantee the independance of the Holy See, they were prepared to envisage some alternative if one could be found. So offensive were such ideas that Cardinal Barnabo at Propaganda in Rome sent a circular letter to the English Bishops in May 1862 in which he complained that "the temporal authority of the Holy See is openly attacked, and the administration of the Papal States, and that it is asserted that Paul III, Paul IV and Pius V preferred temporal emolument to the good of souls and were the cause of England's loss to the Catholic Faith.

The third part of Cardinal Barnabo's letter dealt with "abstruse questions closely connected with the Faith and one of the principal writers often puts forward termerarious and scandalous propositions." This refers to Simpson and his articles on philosophy and religion, and in particular his articles on Faith and Reason in 1861 and a follow up letter written by him under the name DN. Much of Ullathorne's attack on Simpson deals with these articles and as they touch particuarly on Simpson's personal belief it is worth while looking at some of the points raised in a little more detail.

In general the effort made by Simpson was to make the intelligent Catholics of his day think a little harder. He was way ahead of his time for the Bishops of the day considered that laymen should not dabble in theology and that any attempt to give consideration to the views of 'heretics' was equal to the heresy being investigated and would give scandal. Any further attempt to show sympathy with heretics was even worse. In this light the reader can consider the strictures of Bishop Ullathorne referred to earlier.

Bernard Ward in his "Life" of Ullathorne considers correctly that the Bishop totally misunderstood Simpson on most points. Ward says that Simpson was putting forward arguments in favour of the faith from the starting point of a person already well versed in what would then be considered a false philosophical position , particularly that of Kant. Then Simpson goes on to show how Faith and reason are related. Sometimes he uses words which might have been employed by an imaginary opponent and Ullathorne fails to distinguish what is Simpson's real position from that of the imaginary opponent.[8]

McElrath in his Study of Simpson points out that the articles have to be read in the context of the recent appearance of Darwin's *Origin of Species* and *Essays and Reviews*. There was a need to reconcile the findings of modern science with the faith and one must start with the position that faith is concerned with the world of the spirit, while all phenomena belonged to exclusively to the scientific reason and was outside the realm of faith. The essential elements of articles of faith should agree with the fundamental principles and laws of our understanding, that is to say they should be in the truest sense of the word "reasonable", not contrary to reason. With regard to dogma one could distinguish the dogmas themselves and the evidence which made them believable or credible. That element was essentially human and open to reconsideration and development in any age. Indeeed each age has its own philosphy for expressing the essentials of Christianity.

In modern times one might recall the words of Pope John 23rd at the start of the Vatican Council, "The Truths of the Faith are one thing, but the ways of expressing them another, always maintaining the same sense and meaning." I believe that this is exactly what Simpson was trying to say and it marks the difference between the Liberal Catholic Position and that of the later Modernists including Mivart who would accept the first part of the sentence of Pope John but not the second half as they would claim that dogmas themselves take on different meanings in each age. One example of such a difference would be over the key question of the reality of The Resurrection of Christ. Our belief is that a real bodily resurrection took place. The Liberal Catholic might argue about how this took place in the light of our present scientific knowledge, (but would not deny the doctrine) while the modernist may well not accept a bodily resurrection but state that the words of Holy Scripture only refer to the Apostles FAITH in the event, not its reality. But what about particular examples from Simpson's articles themselves.?

In his original article (*Rambler* Sept 1861) Simpson had argued that what he termed 'physical sciences' like geology, when and if directed AGAINST religion have not the same force as sciences which are connected with her origin, her history and her doctrine. Then in his own letter signed DN in the March 1862 Rambler, he clarifies what he means.

> "Physical sciences in themselves are of no religion at all; moral sciences (ie sciences which are directed to the proof of a God or derived from His acts) even when atheistically pursued (ie by one who is determined not to accept the existence of the Divine) become religious in their own way; for even atheism may be made into a dogma, and may become the parent of a whole code of morals. (It would have been better if he had used the word ETHICS here). Moral sciences (ie ethical systems) are never directed to the annihilation of religion but only to its perversion or change, while physical sciences only attack religion accidentally in the points of asserted contact with the world of phenomena. But here they wage a war of extermination; they deny the reality of the contact and they account for the phenomena which religion claims as her own upon merely physical laws, and thus encourage the suspicion that the claims of religion are due only to the imagination of the pious or to the imposture of the cheat."

Now for some reason Bishop Ullathorne took great exception to this passage assuming that the 'dogma' referred to was some how connected with pantheism. What seems far more likely however is that he was referring to say the dogmatic belief of the Catholic in the Real Presence of Christ under the appearances of bread and wine. Clearly one who has no faith might well regard our belief in this matter as a pure superstition.

Ullathorne was however on better ground in criticising another passage from the original September 1861 article where Simpson writes

> "Christians have been always overcome, but always because they have fought for more than the Christian Dogma; because at any given moment they have failed to recognise that all except the central core of revealed truth is human addition and therefore fallible, changeable and obnoxious to decay." and then continuing with the same minimising sentiment. "The Catholic faith then being limited to the invisible substance and the few individual facts in which this substance is manifested, it is clear that the authority of the teacher of faith is by the force of the term comprised within the same limits."

Taken at face value this would surely mean that Simpson is saying that there are very few dogmas in the Catholic Faith and that any other teachings of the Church are open to be changed. This is a dangerous principle and the nearest Simpson gets to complete modernism. Dogmas of faith have many bases, facts etc which lead up to or derive from the dogmas. These we are also bound to believe.

However before condemning Simpson out of hand on this matter, it is worth pointing out that in a long undated letter of 1862 to Charles Meynell he gave Meynell an outline of his personal beliefs and said that the exact spheres of the Church encompassed faith morals and the sacraments, and on these points he would obey and submit even when the Church's decisions were only provisional and not final and therefore not infallible. The church controlled those areas. On other points he would not submit since he did not feel that the sciences were the Church's department."(9)

While perhaps not using the same rather violent language it would seem that the opinion of Bernard Ward in his "Life" of Ullathorne was about right . that is that the Simpson was misunderstood.Simpson wrote:

> "His whole deduction I protest against as unfair, illogical and only to be maintained by garbling my words, applying my sayings to dogmas when I have expressly limited them to evidences, misinterpreting my philosophy of understanding and reason" [10]

He also described Ullathorne's pamphlet as 'knavish imposture' and that Ullathorne was "too great an ass to make one take any pleasure in beating him.."

The *Home and Foreign Review* had a very short life. It closed down in 1864 after the unfavourable reaction of Rome to the Munich Congress of September 1863. A Papal Rescript entitled "Tuas Libenter" criticised the principles which were advocated by Dollinger and his friends including Acton. These principles were much the same as those which influenced the articles in the 'Rambler' and'Home and Foreign'. Soon the famous "Syllabus of Errors" would appear. Acton considered that the right attitude to take would be to combine obedience to the ecclesiastical authority of Rome with however an equal determination to maintain necessary liberty of thought. Acton encouraged Simpson to turn his attention to literary scholarship and so started the final phase of his career.

CHAPTER FIVE
The Final Years

On Acton's advice Simpson now turned his attention to Shakespearean studies. He had already shown an interest in the faith of Shakespeare with some early articles in the *Rambler.* He was the first person to put forward convincing arguments backed up by real scholarship to show that Shakespeare was a life long Catholic rather than merely dying as a Papist. He also made detailed studies of the sonnets and produced a book *An Introduction to the Philosophy of Shakespeare's sonnets* in 1868. However in this essay I am not concerned with the purely literary side of Simpson's career but with his faith.

It is perhaps regrettable that Simpson did not put more work into his recusant studies and Catholic Church History. He did manage though to finish off his "Life of Edmund Campion" which had started off as a series in the *Home and Foreign*, and this was published in 1868. He had also written articles on other martyrs for the *Rambler*, and had thought of trying to continue Dodd's Church History to bring it up to the present time. The Manuscript Book entitled "History" in the Downside Library is all that survives of this endeavour except for articles on Milner which appeared in the *Rambler*. Here is an extract from page 307 probably written around 1863 or 1864. The topic is the role of converts and laity in the Catholic Church.

> "Whenever any question begins to bear upon any ecclesiastical interest or excite attention and party feeling among Catholics, then the clergy have the right of preremptory interference. This view seems to leave to the laity their independence only in matters of no present consequence. In obsolete controversies, questions of art and literature or greater questions on which no present discussion is pending and which do not threaten to become elements of party divisions. The period between 1845 and 1850 witnessed the union of the great mass of clerical converts to the church. They form an element in the Catholic body, a leaven that permeates the mass, but in no sense the party.
> Their influence has not been exercised apart and has rather lent energy to the rising ideas of the true, than of forming the nucleus for a distinct school. Indeed the great bulk of converts entered the church totally incapacitated from taking any real intellectual lead.They were stamped with the zeal of Puseyism, weakened in mind by that sickly system, one sided views advocating foregone conclusions. The converts often tired of their fruitless struggle within the establishment, and crowded into the church with often weary and abject submission to all who look like authority, anxious for a neutral response, and unwilling to ask questions, ready to accept with headlong enthusiasm, anything that could possibly be imagined to be Catholic, to denounce historical criticism,

> enthusiasm, anything that could possibly be imagined to be Catholic, to denounce historical criticism, to be enraptured with everything that proceeded from a Catholic country, to abjure all interest in secular affairs and to prefer any foreign despotism to the English liberties amid which the Church really prospers more than under the paternal care of any autocrat.
>
> On their entrance into the church they were met by the plausible defenders of everything that could be called ultramontane, nursed in the spirit of Roman advocacy, nourished by the glowing and reckless rhetoric of Lammenais and Veuillot."

This is probably a grossly overstated judgment mainly aimed at people like Faber whom he cordially detested but there is certainly an element of truth in what he says.

Simpson is equally scathing about the re-introduction of the Hierarchy in 1850. It failed to live up to its promises.

> "The insane panic which this aggression brought among Protestants did more to secure the unanimity of Catholics in its support than did completeness of the measure itself when reality did not give the whole clergy that fixed position guaranteed by Canon Law which the Cardinal in his appeal to the people of England declares to be the chief object of the measure. In consequence many priests who signed the manifesto for the hierarchy afterwards regretted their act because they did not obtain the canonical system which they asked for (for instance parishes were not set up with security of tenure but rather missions with no such security).
>
> Those who believed it to be a sure means of converting the country have been equally disappointed, as the effect which it had in relations between Catholics and Protestants in England was not precisely what was expected. It repelled instead of attracting. For more than half a century some of the chief dissonances between Protestants and Catholics had been promisingly harmonised. The hospitality given to the French Refugee priests, the alliance of England with the Pope during the great War, the sufferings of Continental Catholics, the revulsion of feeling when the atrocity of penal laws had been brought home to men's minds. The conciliatory spirit of Berrington and Butler, Lingard, Milner and Doyle, Irish Immigration, and

the agitation for emancipation - the unpopularity of the chief enemies of the Catholics.

We were also the chief opponents of reform of all kinds of liberal progress. All these forces went to make up the great movement before which barrier after barrier was falling and was bringing the heart of England closer, nearer to Catholicism . To these we must add special forces like the great movement of renovation and revival which was taking place within the limits of Protestantism and the aesthetic romanticism which directly meant admiration and sympathy to the arts and institutions of the Middle Ages. All this was the broad platform which the Catholicising movement rested on, the whole foundation was laid prior to 1840, even prior to 1836."

Here Simpson is clearly saying that the restoration of the hierarchy in 1850 created the opposite effect to what was intended and in particular the agressive way it was introduced particularly in the famous "Letter from the Flaminian Gate" of Cardinal Wiseman which so incensed public opinion here.

Simpson was asked to fill in the questionnaire sent to leading Catholics to elicit their views on sending Catholics to Oxford and Cambridge. He rejected the idea that Catholics could simply attend on the same conditions as Protestants, so he was very much in favour of a Catholic college set up alongside the existing colleges where Catholic tutors could hold sway. He thought that a Catholic college would be welcome both by Puseyites and Liberals, "The Puseyites even for old friendship's sake; the liberals partly to give a practical proof of their liberality, partly to possess in us a new element of discord."

He did not consider that a good Catholic would have his faith weakened by hearing Protestant views , rather that the student would be fired up to attack such views.

"If Professor A varied his lectures on history with an attack on the Papacy or Professor C turned a lecture on Greek particles into an assault upon dogma, the susceptible minds of Catholic Students would be more likely to take fire with anger than to smoulder with doubt or scruples."

Simpson also consisidered that if students were allowed to attend the infidel University of London why should they be forbidden to attend Oxford, "which so far from being infidel is the Headquarters of the tradition which has preserved whatever remains in Anglicanism of the sacramental and dogmatic principles which have so often during the last 300 years collected young men from Protestant homes and sent them back as Catholics."

Finally he gives a marvellous picture of typical undergraduates of his day which might well fit the 20th or 2lst century just as well.

> "We must not regard the generality of university students as soft, flabby impressionable lumps of unbaked dough. My experience is that they are touchy, turbulent, obstinate, wedded to prejudices in religion, and always more ready to oppose the university authorities than to be tame and passive recipients of any forms imposed upon them."[11]

The events leading to the promulgation of the Infallibility of the Pope at the lst Vatican Council presented Simpson with a problem which he never fully resolved. Before the council he wrote to his friends that he considered Cardinal Manning was near to heresy in claiming the maximum amount of infallibility for the Pope. Manning considered the temporal power of the Pope to be virtually of Divine origin and Simpson rightly thought such an opinion was ridiculous.

At the beginning of 1870 he wrote to the *Times* attacking any possible definition of infallibility and then broadened his position by producing a pamphlet entitled "Papal Infallibility and Persecution; Papal Infallibility and Usury." He claimed the decrees supporting the persecution of heretics made a mockery of infallibility and that the Church's teaching on usury had in fact been altered over the ages. Furthermore that in the questions of persecution and usury the Popes had tried to impose false moral principles upon the whole of Christendom. So neither Acton nor Simpson ever gave the decree even private assent, but agreed between themselves that they would make no public pronouncements about it, and rather "lie low" as it were.

At the time he declared the decree "The Crime of July 18th" and that the fall of Rome which quickly ended the council was a providential revenge. Worst of all though , he took practical action and withdrew his contribution of £25.00 a year to the support of Mitcham Parish, which his family had built up. In today's terms this would be the equivalent of several hundred pounds . On April 1st he wrote to the financial secretary of the Diocese of Southwark.

"I enclose you my contribution for the current half year. At the same time it is proper to say, that if the Bishop of the Diocese should attempt to enforce here any decision which is forced by a mere majority of a council that is not free - if for instance the schema de infallibilitate Papae, I shall not consider myself bound in any way to continue the payment."

After the definition of infallibility was made, he wrote to the Secretary again on October 17th. At that time Southwark was awaiting the appointiment of a successor to Bishop Grant who had died during the council:

> "I can only refer you to my note of April 1st last. The eventuality which I then contemplated has happened, and I no longer feel called upon to make sacrifices for a spiritual authority which shows so little mercy to the consciences of its subjects."

Simpson then withdrew all further support for Mitcham but the payments were started up by his widow after his death.

This might in normal circumstances be considered a rather trifling matter but it is important to note that possibly as a result of the actions of Simpson, the incumbent at Mitcham, Rev Fr. Whyte, died of starvation in 1875!

Simpson was involved in correspondence with Gladstone in 1874 over the latter's pamphlet attacking Catholic allegiance based on the Catholic acceptance of both the Syllabus of Errors of 1864 and the Infallibility decree of 1870. It has been stated that Simpson actually helped Gladstone in preparing this statment but this is most unlikely for the correspondence concerns a particular point where Gladstone has totally misunderstood the Catholic teaching on the Sacramental nature of Christian marriage. Gladstone considered that the Syllabus inferred that the marriage of any Christian of any denomination would be invalid unless held in a Catholic Church. Simpson corrected the great man on this point but added in his own dubious views on how a Catholic could treat of the Infallibility decree.

> "..Only that part of the Council really binds which is protected by anathema. This part simply forbids us to contradict the proposition that the Pope speaking ex cathedra is infallible. It leaves us perfectly free to form our own ideas as to what is ex cathedra, and to collect instances of the Popes writing letters on doctrine to be read in general Councils (like Honorius) and yet writing erroneously. Consequently, such are not ex cathedra. All the difference that I feel since 1870 is that I may no longer publicly contradict a proposition which I may still explain away."

In fact Simpson's position is untenable. A Catholic is held to give both internal and external assent to the Vatican Decree which is itself infallible!

Newman had answered Gladstone in the "Letter to the Duke of Norfolk." Simpson thanked Newman for giving him an honorable mention in connection with his work on Campion.

> "I ought to have written three months ago to thank you for the most kind and generous mention which you made of me in your reply to Gladstone, more especially as I know that you disapproved of the way I spoke of some

Popes in the context of the passage of my life of Campion to which you refer. But the charity you show to men in difficulties is boundless and you will like to to know is most often efficacious. Tomorrow, Admiral Hall, the Secretary for the Admiralty, makes his first Communion. His difficulties were removed by your pamphlet."

It is interesting to note here what Newman thought of Simpson. He wrote to Acton in 1861 (12)

"Further I must though it will pain you, speak out. I despair of Simpson being other than he is. He will always be clever, amusing, brilliant and suggestive. He will always be flicking his whip at Bishops, cutting them in tender places, throwing stones at Sacred Congregations and as he rides along the high road, discharging peashooters at Cardinals who happen by bad luck to look out of the window."

Another eminent person to give an opinion of Simpson was Cardinal Gasquet (13)

"This brilliant writer in many ways undoubtedly one of the ablest of the converts has appeared to many an enigma, to some in past days a scandal, and he is still not infrequently treated as a scapegoat. No one who really knew him or has been through his papers and letters could doubt that in reality he was a true and fervent Catholic. He was daily at Holy Mass and he constantly frequented the sacraments. Whilst some even highly plaed ecclesiastics shrugged their shoulders at La Salette, Simpson simply believed in the apparition. He was exceptionally charitable to those in need. Whenever any one no matter who it was, might be was in trouble, he was as concerned and as anxious to help as if it had been his nearest and deariest friend.

He was misunderstood by many but it is impossible not to confess that the misunderstanding was mainly the result of his own methods. His transparent sincerity, his ready forgiveness of injuries and his fredom from all animosity against those who bullied and slandered him seem worthy of notice here.

He had the gift, the fatal gift it may be called in the circumstances of catching the comical side of serious matters which made him not always a respecter of persons

> matters which made him not always a respecter of persons in authority, accustomed to look for reverence and obedience..by nature he loved to tease but certainly not to hurt, and some ecclesiastics especially some dignified ecclesiastics seemed to possess a special power of evoking in him this peculiar spirit."

Simpson was often ill in the last few years and in spite of the difficulties he had with some local priests he received the last rites at least once at Clapham in 1872. This was probably the onset of the stomach cancer which finally carried him off in 1876. It is a pity that his diaries are lost or destroyed. Only that for 1875 survives and there are gaps in it which may be accounted for by illness. The entries show meetings with his friends like Acton, Wetherall and Renouf and a close involvement in local affairs. In 1875 he became a magistrate and he was also involved with the local Parish vestry and poor law relief.

Unaware that he was dying of cancer he decided to visit Rome for the Easter of 1876. When he arrived at the end of March Simpson became very ill and asked for the last rites. When the priest came he was already unable to even speak or receive Communion. He died at 11.00 in the morning on Wednesday 5th April and was buried in complete anonymity in "an obscure niche in the Roman cemetery of San Lorenzo."

NOTES AND SOURCES

In this essay the main biographical information has been taken from the biography by Fr. Damien McElrath. Other sources are quoted directly. Simpson's output was phenomenal but regrettably it was always in the form of magazine articles, even the Shakespeare material. There is a mass of unpublished material in the Downside Library collection of papers for future scholars to peruse.

NOTES

1) All this material from McElrath, Damien. O.F.M. *Richard Simpson* published at Louvain 1972.
2) Southwark Archives - Universities of Oxford and Cambridge file.
3) Downside Library - Simpson Papers
4) All this is from the 1846 Diary of the journey to Rome in the Downside Library collection
5) Simpson to Hecker quoted by McElrath page 59
6) The series of articles started in July 1855.
7) Altholz J.L. and McElrath D. and Holland J.C. *Correspondence of Lord Acton and Richard Simpson*, 3 vols 1971
8) Butler, Abbot Cuthbert O.S.B. *Life and Times of Bishop Ullathorne*, 2 vols. London 1926. See Vol 1 p 309ff for a full discussion of the differences between Simpson and Ullathorne over the Rambler.
9) Quoted by McElrath page 91
10) Quoted by McElrath page 95
11) Southwark Diocesan Archives- Universities of Oxford and Cambridge.files
12) Ward,Wilfred. *Life of John Henry Cardinal Newman*. 2 Vols London 1912. vol 2 page 529
13) Gasquet; *Lord Acton and His Circle*..page xiiv.

PART FIVE
St. George Jackson Mivart
Towards Final Apostasy

INTRODUCTION

To call Mivart an Oxford Convert is something of a misnomer. He was indeed all set to go to Oxford but became a Catholic a couple of months before he was due to enter and as a Catholic was debarred.

He is however a convert resulting directly from the movement and on that ground is worthy to be included in these essays. He takes us right to the opposite extreme from the Ultramontane Coffin by ending up as a total modernist, even in 20th century terms a neo modernist.

There is an existant biography by Gruber which was published in America and is hard to find over here. Furthermore he concentrates on Mivart's work as a biologist and zoologist. In this essay as with the others I am concerned with the development of his faith rather than his career. Unlike the other figures in this volume, the really interesting developments take place only in the last 30 years of his life and so the first part of this essay will deal quickly with his earlier years.

CHAPTER ONE.
Earliest Years, until 1874

St George Jackson Mivart was born on November 30th 1827 at 34 Brook St, Grosvenor Square, London. His father was James Edward Mivart a man of means, who founded Mivart's Hotel later better known as Claridge's. He was a man of literary tastes endowed also with a love of music. His mother was Caroline Georgina Cuningham of mixed Scots and Irish descent. She was had a strong religious bias and also a love of literature. She became a Catholic herself in 1846.

St George as a name he acquired directly from his

godfather St George Caulfield, and he was the youngest of four children. His first school was kept by certain ladies living in Edwardes Square London, and then later he attended an establishment run by a Mr Dempster at Turnham Green where he spent about three years. He was evidently extremely precocious. At the age of ten he was a regular theatre goer and had already made a visit to Paris with his parents.

After leaving Mr Dempster's academy he was sent to a Dr Laing in Clapham who started him on Greek and Latin. He was slightly eccentric in that the pupils had to eat pudding first and the meat course last.

At this stage of his life he started what would be his life long interest in biology and zoology. At home he was it seems fascinated by his fathers copy of Buffon's *Histoire Naturelle Generale et Particuliere*. This was an original edition of 1749 in 38 folio volumes. The work contains a large number of plates depicting animals and their anatomy. Young St George asked his father to translate sections from the volumes when he had time. It was his father also who introduced him to the London Zoological Gardens as he was already in 1836 a member of the zoological Society. At the Gardens he met two of his father's friends called Yarrell and Gould who presented him with obejcts of biological interest to furnish a little museum. In particular Gould presented him with Australian bird skins. He later added to his collection by visiting Steven's auction rooms with his father to collect reptiles preserved in spirits. These he later presented to Stonyhurst College.

At the very end of his life Mivart contributed an article to the *Weekly Register* (Nov 18th 1899) in which he lists the books that have most influenced him. First and foremost was the Buffon, in particular because to some extent it paved the way for Darwin and Huxley. The other two books were Gibbon's *Decline and Fall of the Roman Empire* and T.F. Dibdin's *Bibliographical, Antiquarian, and Picturesque Tour in France and Germany* of 1829. He made the same journey as Dibdin himself in 1884 and the

Weekly Register article gives several amusing anecdotes of his trip. At Kremsmunster Abbey near Linz he found a staircase with "upwards of 100 numbered portraits of former pupils in powdered wigs. Unfortunately the corresponding list (of their names) was lost during the Napoleonic wars. It was to me to very sad sight to see this multitude of young faces about which no one knew anything, not even a name - life like shadows of forgotten dead!" At Melk Abbey" High Mass was not liturgical; no introit, offertory, sequence or communion was sung by the choir which was in the western gallery and the music was very florid"

To return to our narrative, in 1839 Mivart was despatched to Clapham Grammar School kept by the Rev Charles Pritchard, later a distinguished Oxford Professor. Here at least the meat came before the pudding, and bread cheese and beer formed the evening repast. Pritchard introduced biology as a class to supplement the scholastic diet of classics and mathematics. Mivart also developed a taste for fine church architecture and visited St. George's Southwark then still in the early stages of construction. About 1841 he spent a couple of terms at Harrow under Dr. Wordsworth but returned in the autumn to Clapham because of poor health.

At this time the family were attending St Mark's North Audley Street where a Mr Wingfield was curate and a strong Tractarian. Wingfield's sister later married W.G. Ward. The families became friendly. With Ward and Wingfield they attended the afternoon service at the Margaret Street Chapel where Oakeley "hobbled up the pulpit steps for the sermon but at that time the only ritualistic development was two lighted candles on the communion table."[1]

In an article for the *Dublin Review* on "Conversion of England" written in July 1884 he adds a little more.

"The writer (ie Mivart) well recollects being taken as a boy by the late Dr. Ward and his brother in law Mr Wingfield to evensong at Margaret St Chapel then renowned for its surplice clad preacher, Mr Oakeley, its pair of lighted candles on the communion table and its popish collecting bags to receive the congregation's offerings."

By now his parents were worried about his friendship with the popish Wingfield so they sent their son to a private tutor called Davies, an Anglican Divine of little merit it would seem, for he was unable to argue against the Catholic doctrines put to him by his young pupil. Hoping to improve matters, his parents moved him to King's College but here he resided with a Dr. Brewer who professed to hold all the Roman doctrines except Papal Supremacy. Now Mivart increased his Catholic reading with Milner's *End of Religious Controversy* which so influenced Sibthorp before him. Another book he devoured was *A Plea for the Revival of Christian Architecture and the Present State of Christian Architecture in England* by Pugin. So impressed was he by this latter tome that he set off on a tour of the many Catholic Churches then being built. He also read the famous prayer book the *Garden of the soul* and started saying the "Memorare" prayer daily. Eventually he came to Birmingham where St. Chad's was being built and met up with Fr. Moore who asked him if he were a Catholic and received the reply "I hardly know". Moore took him to see the sisters of Mercy at Handsworth, then the Church at Cheadle, one of Pugin's finest, and also Alton Towers, the home of Lord Shrewsbury recently extended by Pugin and now better known as an amusement park. A trip was also arranged to St Barnabas at Nottingham then being built with money provided by Sibthorp. On April llth 1844 he came to Oscott and on May l9th attended his final Protestant Service. He delayed his final reception a few days to please his mother but was finally taken into the fold of Rome on June 2nd by Fr. Moore. Back home in London he was presented to the Jesuit Fr. Brownbill who received Simpson in the following year. Brownbill became his first regular confessor.

In October he went into residence at Oscott with a view

to trying his vocation but only stayed just over a year. But what a year. While he was there he witnessed the reception of all the major Tractarian converts who at least passed through the college where Wiseman was Rector. His fellow students included the future Lord Acton, Peter le Page Renouf, friend of Simpson and Liberal Catholic, George Talbot who later became Bishop's agent in Rome and Amherst the Historian who later became Bishop of Northampton. It seems Mivart was particularly friendly with Amhurst. Renouf was appointed his tutor but Mivart considered him a poor teacher, but one who introduced him to Fichte and Kant...which may indicate the early beginnings of the liberal thinking which caused his final downfall. He was also very fond of Fr. George Spencer just as Sibthorp had been. He joined a voluntary group under Spencer which recited the entire office every day. Later in his Dublin Review article he writes:

> "Dear and beloved George Spencer. Holy venerated Father Ignatius!Who that recollects your tender kindness, your delicate consideration for the feelings of others, who were so often wanting in consideration for you, your wonderful patience, your unexampled humility, your carefully hidden self-denial, your untiring zeal for souls and above all your unceasing lifelong prayer for the conversion of your country,; who can doubt that sooner or later you will find your place upon the Church's Altars and receive publicly that homage and veneration which have long been privately paid you by those privileged to know you well and whose consciences were for too brief a space, subject to your wise, gentle and loving sway."

It is only in this century that Mivart's wishes have started to be realised with the introduction of his cause.

Mivart remained at Oscott until December 1845 and thus witnessed the arrival of all the main Tractarian Converts including Newman, Ward, Oakeley and many others. However he had then determined not to become a priest and in January 1846 became a student at Lincoln's Inn.

He was called to the bar on 30th January 1851 but never practiced.

Instead he turned to a scientific career. He studied biology and zoology privately mainly under the guidance of Professor Huxley. These are more or less the hidden years in his life for it was not until after 1858 that he started writing. What we do know is that from 1849 he was a member of the Royal Institution, and from 1858 a fellow of the Zoological Society. By 1862 he was sufficiently well established in his own right to be appointed lecturer in comparative anatomy at St Mary's Hospital London. At this time he started writing a series of learned articles about the skeletal anatomy of primates. Such essays as "The Osteology of the Insectivora" were hardly likely to bring him fame, but in 1869 a long essay entitled "The Appendicular Skeleton of the Primates" was considered of such merit that he was elected a Fellow of the Royal Society. Later he became a fellow of the Linnean Society serving as vice-president in 1892.

What took him into the limelight in Catholic circles was his reply to Darwin's *Origin of Species*. In 1871 he produced a short book entitled *On the Genesis of Species*. This was an effort to show that evolution could be squared up with the Catholic teaching on creation.

He already had become friendly with Cardinal Manning especially as both were members of the metaphysical society along with other leading figures of the day such as Huxley, Gladstone and Ruskin. Manning secured for him a PhD degree from Pope Pius IX. It is however important to note that these awards did not imply that the Holy Father had actually read the works in question that prompted the awards, merely that he was doing a favour to the Bishop who put a particular name forward. So what exactly did Mivart teach in this book and in the follow up pamphlet *Evolution and its Consequences* published originally in the Contemporary Review for January 1872.

Although he accepted the theory that man's body might evolve from a sub human species, he was clear to point out the essential disparity between the highest faculties of brute animals and the power of human reason in man. He also refused to accept that organic and inorganic matter were essentially the same, and though he accepted natural selection (survival of the strongest), he did not give it a prominent place in his system. As an evolutionist he regarded species change as inherent in nature but his view of evolution is based on the existence of a first cause which could be proven on rational grounds as an ordering intelligence pervading the universe. So Evolution works through the natural law. Evolution however cannot account for the intellectual aspect of man and the soul of man must be distinct in its nature from the body. To back up his theories he invoked the aid of theology thus starting what in fact was to become a main concern of the rest of his life and the factor that led to his final apostasy, for he was in no way a trained theologian. Huxley attacked his teaching and Mivart replied in the *Quarterly Review* article.

Mivart believed that the theologian Suarez admitted principles which were compatible with evolution and Scholastic Philosophy while not personally holding the theory of evolution itself. Furthermore although granting that the Fathers had all accepted the relatively small age of the universe, Mivart stated that St Augustine spoke of all the creation referred to in the Book of Genesis taking place in one instant "potentially and causally", and this would accord with development of species and slow evolution. In the pamphlet he also goes to great lengths to explain the freedom that Catholics have in interpreting the "Six days of Creation" He also deals with the problem of the infusion of the human soul referring back to St.Thomas·Aquinas who taught that the embryo first received a vegetative, then an animal and finally a human soul. For Adam, Mivart seems to posit that he might have received a human soul after his birth.

Mivart then can be taken as the first person to put forward the position which is accepted generally by

Catholics today that the creation of man's soul can be separated from the evolution of his body. Simpson had been groping towards a coherent theory but Mivart is the first to put it forward both scientifically and theologically.

However from 1872 onwards Mivart's religious progress was nearly all downhill till his death.[1]

CHAPTER TWO*Trying to reconcile science and religion*

We know very little of Mivart's private life. He married round about 1860 and they had one son Frederick, who became a Doctor. In his turn he had one son who was killed in the 1914-1918 war and thus the family line is extinct to the best of my knowledge. He lived most of the time in London in order to be near his work at St.Mary's Hospital but as certain letters of his are addressed from first Uckfield and later Chilworth, one may presume these residences were in the nature more of country retreats. After 1886 he seems to have permanently resided in London principally at No 77 Inverness Terrace. When in town he attended St Francis Church, Ogle Street and was a great benefactor to that Church. He also helped the Little Sisters at Hammersmith and at various times was secretary of the Catholic Union and warden of the Guild of St Luke for the study of Christian Antiquities and True princples of Art. He inherited from Fr. George Spencer an intense desire for the conversion of England, at least until the very last period of his life, and was very anxious to promote the cause of the English Martyrs.

On the 18th May 1879 he wrote to Bishop Dannel of Southwark from Uckfield:

> "I do hope I shall have your approval in trying to interest laymen in an effort to expedite the canonisation of our English Martyrs. I hope also you will approve a further effort to obtain a permission for your diocese to keep a feast of St John of Rochester ie. Cardinal Fisher. I have been gathering information about the process and find it is complete and includes all our martyrs together, a work saving great trouble and expense and more likely to succeed because miracles if found will do for all. I also

find that though more than 200 Japanese martyrs were beatified at one time and in one process yet this has not prevented the Society obtaining permission to keep no less than eleven feasts of those among them that belong to the Society"[2]

In 1883 he met Edmund Bishop, well known Catholic Historian and colleague of Cardinal Gasquet in his historical research. They became close friends and corresponded regularly right up to the end of Mivart's life. To start with their meetings concerned the plans to rebuild Buckfast Abbey but later they discussed theological points which were worrying Mivart. In the early letters at the end of 1883 and the start of 1884 he discusses plans he is making with Fr.Ryan of Ogle St. to improve the liturgy there. On the 23 Dec 1883 he writes to Bishop:

"He has I may tell you confidentially expressed a strong desire to make his church one specially distinguished for its ritual. He is I think, quite disposed to be taught and has very exceptional opportunities with his boys and gentry. I think we might do some real good there, we might perhaps introduce Terce".

On the 5th Jan 1884 he writes again" have seen Fr Ryan and he is going to begin at once about the Creed and the Asperges. He spontaneously suggested the printing of a little Book, very few pages, to give the parts to be sung in Latin and English with directions when to stand, kneel and sit."

In that same year 1884 he wrote the article on the Conversion of England for the *Dublin Review* already referred to. The article is very perceptive. Rather like Simpson in his "History notes" he tries to analyse the reasons why the conversion of England did not take place after the ending of the Tractarian movement. He alleges a drop off in the number of converts, the rise of a liberal spirit of morality, the rise of agnosticism in intellectual circles. As to Catholic matters he complains of too much Italianate devotion and not enough psalmody, he wishes to see a limited introduction of the vernacular into the Liturgy. There would be more conversions if Catholics in general showed a higher moral tone than the majority amongst whom they lived. The clergy and laity need a better education particularly in scientific matters. The laity should be expected to assist the priests in spreading the Gospel. He suggested the idea of dedicated laymen who might take over particularly the financial chores. He suggests that parish priests were having to leave pastoral work to their curates."

Clearly he would have been delighted by the Vernacular of today's Mass but the same complaints about lack of lay involvement in the real work of parishes are still made at the end of the 20th century.

Mivart was writing almost continuously right up to 1893 a series of learned works of anatomy. Most of these were produced for the zoological society. One work in particular however should be noted. In 1881 he wrote a monograph entitled "The Cat - An Introduction to the study of back boned Animals especially Mammals" The Dictionary of National Biography says of this work "For fullness and accuracy of detail and lucidity of exposition is worthy to rank with Huxley's "Crayfish" However the minute detail into which Mivart goes on every part of the anatomy of the cat has led it to be considered one of the most boring books of the century, of interest only to the most avid lover of furry felines.

From 1874 onwards though he turned his attention towards philosophy and Psychology and this led eventually to his total lack of faith. I have stated already that 1874 marked a turning point. It marked the final ending of Mivart's friendship with Darwin and Huxley.

Already relations with Darwin were strained as a result of his criticism of the *Origin of Species*.Darwin is reported to have spent sleepless nights reflecting on the criticisms. But in 1874 he attacked in print Huxley's son for allegedly teaching immorality in connection with marriage and divorce. The accusations were false and due to a misunderstanding of what Huxley junior was saying. Mivart was asked to apologise but his so called apology made matters worse. From that time onwards neither Darwin nor Huxley would speak to Mivart except on essential business. Furthermore as a direct result Mivart suffered a fate almost worse than death itself, he was blackballed for admission to the Athaneum club.

Although in 1876 he was awarded the honorary degree of PhD by the Holy Father he suffered a further setback due to the failure of the short lived Catholic University. This was set up in 1875 at Manning's instigation in order to provide University education for the sons of Catholic gentry unable to enter Oxford or Cambridge. It was however a half hearted measure. Manning left the management to Mgr Capel who was already running a school at Kensington. Capel was far more interested in the school than the University. The hierarchy did not provide enough money to run it properly and worse still, Capel proved a complete charlatan, diverting funds towards the school and into his own pocket. The university seems never to had more than 20 pupils and most of these were of very low grade intelligence.An exception however must be made of one very distinguished pupil who later became Abbot Cuthbert Butler of Downside. Even he seems only to have stayed for about a year. The staff chosen were excellent including Paley and Mivart himself. Mivart had the chair of biology at £600 per annum, a not inconsiderable amount for the time,and the largest salary of all the professors. But he was appalled at the way operations were conducted and does not seem to have stayed on to the bitter end.

The first of his works to cause real unease was yet another follow up to the *Genesis of Species* entitled *Contemporary Evolution* and published in 1876. Parts of this work are quite orthodox or at least not specifically unorthodox.

> "As the process of evolution has gone on..so the evolution of humanity has proceded and is proceding

from direct and simple conscious apprehensions to more and more reflex self-conscious and complex apprehensions. And this applies fully to the acceptance of the Christian Church. As it has been, so it will be. Of time there is no stint..by the continuance of the evolutionary process there is to be plainly discerned in the distant future a triumph of the church compared with which that of medieval Christendom was but a transient adumbration. A triumph brought about by moral means alone by the slow process of exhortation, example and individual conviction after every error has been freely propagated and every denial freely made and every rival system provided with a free field for its display. A triumph infinitely more glorious than any brought about by the sword and fulfilling at last the old pre Christian prophecies of the Kingdom of God on earth."[3]

So far this is acceptable if somewhat optimistic. Mivart seems to be saying that man's intellect itself is evolving and improving all the time and that it is only a matter of time before all will see the light of Christ's Gospel. Clearly the weakness is that he finds no room for God's grace. But after this we find serious problems arising.

> "This must be based on a recognition of the absolute right to the free exercise of one's conscience, the right of each man freely to perform such actions as God THROUGH HIS CONSCIENCE has enjoined him to perform provided they do not deprive other men of similar freedom to fulfill what they believe to be their duty."

Gruber suggests that this thought is influenced by Newman's Apologia and the "Letter to the Duke of Norfolk" but surely it is going way beyond Newman's teaching on conscience. Mivart's idea of the supremacy of conscience is such that no power on earth (nor presumably Divine Grace which is never mentioned) has any power whatever to influence one's conscience. The end result will be individualism, every man is his own religion. This will be the position that Mivart actaully takes up at the end of his life. Mivart appears to also to merge free will and intellect as if they were one operation. The free will eventually emerges from the free intellect. The idea that men would one day be led to the truth purely through developed intellectual powers is Utopian anyway in the light of the Fall.

W.G.Ward in the Dublin Review launched into the attack against Mivart.Ward accused Mivart of taking up the same position as Simpson and the reader will have noted points of similarity from the passage quoted here, with Simpson's own writing. Ward also pointed out that it was wrong to allow atheists and others to propagate their own views about marriage because such views would serve to corrupt the ignorant, the untutored and the young. In this he has been shown to be absolutely correct for as the laws of the land have lost their Christian basis on moral matters, so there has indeed been a widespread increase in immoral behaviour. Ward however as so often goes over the top:

> "Surely one must recognise the necessity of repression by force if necessary, of anyone or anything which threatens through opposition the absolute ideal which the state has taken as its own ? To do otherwise would be to risk the loss of truth and the triumph of error"

Such a view of course would suggest he was in favour of religious persecution provided it was practiced by Christians.[4]

Mivart answered Ward in the May issue of the Dublin Review.

> "Reason possesses no freedom of choice, but is compelled to follow evidence. No authority can be accepted in defiance of Reason. Authority can be justified only by Reason and cannot therefore be justified if it opposes Reason."

Mivart was to experience just such an event when he was excommunicated at the end of his life and his reaction was quite predictable in the light of what he says here.[3]

Newman wrote to Mivart at this time:

> "You must not be surpised at finding yourself the

object of criticism in consequence of passages of your book...Those who would not allow Galileo to reason 300 years ago will not allow any one else now;..their notion of stability in faith is ever to be repeating errors and then repeating retractions of them." [5]

Over the next few years he diverted his attention somewhat towards pure philosophy blended with a little psychology. He published a collection of his philosophical writing in two works, *Lessons from Nature as manifested in Mind and Matter* (1876) and *Nature and Thought* an attempt to refute the philosophy of Berkely. He started to explore the relation between sensuality and intellectual powers.

"When these traits are compared with those of the lower mental faculty, the basis of distinction between the sentient and the intellectual nature of man becomes clear. The characterisation of the intellectual faculty of man consists of a series of propositions all of which are based upon the primary philosophical assumption of a real world apart from, and existing independently of, the sentient experiencing organism."

For Mivart the rationality of the human mind allows it to transcend the world of immediate experience and perceive by its (divine) nature the eternal reality which is the world of God and from which stem those higher virtues, those absolutes towards which man was created to strive. Once again the intellect seems to be doing all the work without the direct help of God's grace.

From around 1884 Mivart turned his attention to Biblical criticism. He had at that time been in correspondence with Newman over various issues. He considered that Catholics had various grievances with the Government and thought it might be a good idea to have public prayers for the blessing of God on State authorities recited in all Catholic Churches. Newman urged caution on that issue reminding Mivart it was only 20 years before his (ie Newman's) time that Dr Challoner died of fright following from the Gordon Riots.

"While then I feel as keenly as you do the state of

English Catholics socially and think it our duty to improve it, I doubt whether insisting on small grievances is the way to raise it.I more than fear that little can be done in our (or rather your) day." [6]

Mivart then wrote to Newman on May 9th that year asking for his views on the relationship of modern scientific discovery with the teaching of the Church. He received a very cautious reply: "How can priests and confessors give up what is received by Catholic Tradition without some better grounds for surrendering it than they have?... What is the good of argument unless opponents combat a man of science, when the latter virtually denies the possibility of miracles and the former holds that the most stupendous have actually occurred?" Newman circumvents this problem and does not want to be drawn in. [7]

In July 1885 Mivart started writing regularly for the secular journal "Ninetheeth Century". His first article was entitled "Modern Catholics and Scientific Freedom." In 1887 came "The Catholic Church and Biblical Criticism" while in 1889 he published a short book entitled "On Truth, a Systematic Enquiry". He described this to Edmund Bishop as: "..philosophical but my endeavour has been to make it plain and simple and not at all controversial. It only deals with the prolegomena of faith..it starts by professing to be an enquiry for truth. I am troubled about a title and incline to take as one the question "What is Truth ?" Prophetic indeed as for the next ten years he would asking that very question about Biblical truth. But first of all came the real bombshell, an article reprinted as a pamphlet entitled. "Happiness in Hell." The consequences were dire indeed.

CHAPTER THREE *Happiness in Hell*

The Article *Happiness in Hell* is probably Mivart's best known work after *Genesis of Species* mainly of course for the surprising title. During my seminary training many years ago Mivart came up as a minor figure in Church

History. He was dismissed as an eminent biologist who in later life went mad and wrote a pamphlet called *Happiness in Hell* for which he was excommunicated and died outside the Church. This was a gross over-simplification. The true facts are those which will appear in this narrative.

The article itself first appeared in *Nineteenth Century* in December 1892 and with two follow up papers entitled *THE Happiness in Hell* and *Last words on Happiness* in Hell",it was placed on the Index of Prohibited Books in July 1893. Here are some of the key extracts. First of all Mivart gives us the underlying thinking behind publication. It is pure modernism, about ten years ahead of Tyrrell.

> "Each age has its own peculiarities of thought and temper. As it has hitherto been, so it will probably continue to be. Therefore not only must some statements of historical facts be more credible at one time than another, but some declarations of doctrine must be more sympathetically welcomed or found more repugnant to the prevailing temper in one century than in another; therefore any revelation intended to last for future ages must be made known in terms and symbols some of which will constitute difficulties to its reception at one time and others at another time. It will be amply sufficient if in each age it can be..reconciled with that ages knowledge and dominant sentiment."

Mivart here seems almost to be saying that some doctrines can be played down or rephrased if they seem difficult for one particular age to accept. He continues:

> "The Christian Church makes no claim to inspiration but only to such guidance as shall ultimately and often at the last moment save it from falling into fatal error in authoritatively deciding questions of faith and morals. Such mere assistance in no way dispenses Popes and councils from making use of every available means for arriving at the truth.It is quite clear that on Catholic principles they may fail to rise adequately to an occasion which presents itself and though so far assisted as to avoid fatal error may occasion more or less detriment to the domains of physical science, politics and aesthetics, and so for a time impair temporal progress."

When one has cut through the verbiage of this statement it would appear that Mivart is teaching that the Church must always change its tack on scientific matters otherwise it will be always be seen as a backward looking force. Mivart is putting forward exactly the same ideas for matters of doctrine also.

Athough technically out of due order I now quote the entire final paragraph of the document which summarises the teachings given. For a more detailed coverage of the arguments we can consider how they were approached by Dr.R.F.Clarke in his official reply. First though Mivart's words:

"God has with infinite benevolence but with inscrutable purposes created human beings, the overwhelming majority of whom being incapable of grave sin, attain to an eternity of unimaginable natural happiness, the utmost of which their nature is capable and which includes a natural knowledge and love of God. (ie what we call Limbo). Another multitude undergo a certain probation on earth and attain to a further state exactly proporationed to their merits or demerits which may equal or fall short of the natural happiness of those incapable of sin. (Presumably he means purgatory but it is hardly a definition in line with the Church's teaching).

God has further endowed a certain number of mankind with faculties whereby they are rendered capable of a supernatural union with Him, a bliss which in this life they can neither imagine or really desire, though they may aspire to it as a good beyond their power to picture.

This privilege carries with it a dread risk of failure resulting in the loss of supernatural happiness. But this failure may be of all degrees with corresponding divergencies of condition. Yet for the very worst in spite of the positive and unceasing suffering..existence is acceptable and is by them preferred to non existence while we are permitted to believe in an eternal upward progress though never attaining to the supernatural state which would be most unwelcome and repugnant to such souls. They are left to themselves in those various inferior conditions which they have made theirs by their own choice and which they have led themselves to persist in

> and prefer. Thus the hell even of the positively damned who have forfeited grace bestowed may yet be regarded as a place which God has from all eternity prepared for those who will not accept the higher goods offered by Him for their acceptance. Hell in its widest sense namely as including all those blameless souls who do not enjoy that vision, must be considered as for them an ABODE OF HAPPINESS transcending all our most vivid anticipations, so that man's natural capacity for happiness is there GRATIFIED TO THE VERY UTMOST. Nor is it even possible for the Catholic Theologian of the most severe and rigid school to deny that thus considered, there is and there will for all eternity be a REAL AND TRUE HAPPINESS IN HELL. (The final words are in capitals in Mivart's text...the other capitals I have added).

In the event Mivart has corrupted the Church's teaching on purgatory as well as on hell, in finding that there is happiness all round. But for the condemnation R.F.Clarke who was given the task of replying to the article pinpointed three particular errors.

First; condition of the damned in hell is one of evolution and gradual amelioration. Many of the Fathers held that a mitigation of their sufferings is vouchsafed to them from time to time and theologians of weight recognise this as a tenable opinion.

Second; The damned find in hell a certain harmony with their own mental condition as it were and hug their chains esteeming as preferable those lower activities and desires which had been their choice and solace here on earth.

Third. For all the lost (ie damned), existence is better than non existence and St. Augustine distinctly affirms that they prefer their existence as damned souls to non existence. Mivart also tells us that when Catholic theologians draw the most awful pictures of hell, they are merely bringing out the inconceivable distance between the satisfactions of this lower condition and the joys of heaven.

To reply to this Clarke shows that the quotations from the Fathers as used by Mivart are incomplete and that a full examination of the texts shows that they often teach the opposite. For instance the idea that people in hell might prefer existence to non existence is certainly not taught by Augustine. What he refers to is that here on earth we mortals always prefer to hang on to life rather than wish to see it end . That is as a general rule of course, for those who commit suicide etc certainly are prefering non-existence to existence.

The idea that a respite is allowed for a time to the lost, as for instance when Christ descended into hell, is based on Petavius who quotes from St. John Chrysostom and Prudentius. Petavius however having given quotes which support that position taken from these fathers concludes by saying. "The opinion (of a respite allowed for a time to the lost) is not to be lightly brushed aside as an absurdity THOUGH IT IS OPPOSED TO THE GENERAL AGREEMENT OF CATHOLICS AT THE PRESENT DAY."

Mivart fails to quote the words given in capitals here.

Clarke concluded his reply with standard Catholic doctrine.

> "The fear of hell is a powerful deterrent to many educated as well as uneducated people, and many a sin would be committed were it not for the wholesome dread of eternal misery before the sinners eyes. For this reason I cannot help regarding Professor Mivart's teaching as very mischevious as well as false." (8)

Mivart in his immediate comeback wrote that that he had been assured by an American priest the one great obstacle to the conversion of America was the moral disapproval so generally felt to the doctrine of hell as commonly understood ,and he felt it his duty to try and clear the road in the direction he had done. He wrote "It is with much satisfaction and deep thankfulness that I look back on the destruction of superstitions as to the origin of species and of man, the age of the world, the universality of the deluge, the authorship and date of various canonical books and last and not least, the nature of the torments in Hell in which I though unworthy have been permitted to play a modest part."

Once again in this reply we can see the degree to

which modernism was affecting his thinking. If certain doctrines are unnaceptable in the present age, we can re-interpret them or water them down until they become acceptable.

When the condemnation of his writings came out and they were placed upon the index of forbidden books in July 1893 Mivart submitted but told his friends that having a book placed on the index in no way stopped him from continuing to hold the views promoted in it. He had not been formally excommunicated so he could go on just as before. In order to justify his new position he wrote a further article entitled "The Index and my Articles" In this 'Apologia' we read:

> "I have ever been exclusively guided by what appeared to me to be the dictates of calm and solid reason. I have also been habitually possessed by a strong desire to probe questions to their ultimate foundations and as a consequence have arrived at the conclusion that all knowledge whatever, must rest upon the power of our intellect to apprehend (a) certain ultimate facts, (b) certain necessary principles, and (c) certain valid processes of reasoning. If the certainty of these facts principles and processes be denied or even really doubted, we are logically reduced to a state of mental paralysis, whereby not only all religious belief but all physical science also, become logically impossible." and later on ; "It has long been evident to me that an enormous mass of ignorance and prejudice hides from a multitude of well meaning men, the goodness, beauty and truth of the Catholic faith. Therefore I have again and again endeavoured to diminish such ignorance and prejudice by pointing out the harmony which really exists between Catholicity and Science, both physical and historical."

At the end he makes a profession of his faith in the Catholic Church and refuses to contemplate rejoining the Anglican Communion. He accepts Papal Infallibility. "The Church of Rome however does assert itself to possess not only absolute but also infallible authority and that without being inspired, it is nevertheless so assisted by the Divine Spirit, that its Supreme Head, the Pope, when he teaches ex- Cathedra cannot fall into error as regards either faith or morals."

The trouble was that Mivart could never understand the role of the ordinary magisterium of the Church. While prepared to accept the occasional "ex Cathedra" pronouncement, he regarded practically any other statement emanating from the Holy Father or the congregations as decidedly fallible if not downright erroneous.

In that same year Pope Leo XIII published his encyclical letter "Providentissimus Deus" on Biblical Criticism and Inspiration. This marks the start of the Papal comeback against creeping modernism though the main thrust had to wait until Pius X issued his famous encyclical "Pascendi" and the list of errors in "Lamentabili".

For Mivart it spelt the end of his dreams. He developed an absolute obsession about inspiration or rather as he saw it, the lack of inspiration in the sacred writers when they propounded unhistorical facts like the Tower of Babel and the Flood. But for the time being Mivart remained quiet, unwilling to face the wrath of Rome again. In 1898 he could write to Edmund Bishop:

> "If we have to say the Bible is verbally inspired and in all its parts and is practically written by the finger of God (Vatican decree and the Encyclical), then it is very difficult to be at all comfortable. As to the account of creation, God need not have written such misleading words as 'and the evening and morning were the first, second, third day etc.' Neither need he have said that the grass and the trees existed before the sun and moon..These statements are absolutely false.I shall be told that it is the Church which has to decide what the Scriptures mean. But the whole authority of the Church rests on Scripture for if there is one thing certain it is that the earliest Christian teachers and propagandists appealed to the scriptures as THE PROOF of their religious truth." (9)

In 1899 the Index of Prohibited books was reissued and Mivart wrote at once to the congregation when he dicovered his own works were still found there. He asked why he had been denounced and who was responsible. The reply told him simply that he had been censured by the Holy Office. On receiving this reply Mivart withdrew his submission and the scene was set for the terrible events of the next twelve months.

CHAPTER FOUR
Excommunication, Death, Burial and reburial

Before looking at some of the letters of this final period of Mivart's life it is interesting to see that he became involved in the famous Dreyfus case. Most Catholics in France supported the moves against Dreyfus possibly because he was a Jew. When they were proved wrong and Dreyfus vindicated there was an outburst of anti-Catholic feeling both in France and England. Mivart wrote to the *Times* on October 17th 1899,

> "The Bishops especially have disgraced themselves in a deplorable manner by their toleration of the vilest newspapers and the bestowal of their imprimatur on publications, the iniquity of which is only exceeded by their marvellous absurdity...How can the Pope condemn flagrant injustice when his mouth is closed by the flagrant injustice of his own special agents, the Roman Congregations..consisting of men who have obtained more or less of what most men care for, influence, power and some ways and means."

A whole century later the same attacks are being made by those opposed to Roman decisions.

At the start of the year 1900 matters reached a head. Mivart wrote two articles *The Continuity of Catholicism* and *Some recent apologists* The first appeared in "Nineteenth Century" and the latter in the *Fortnightly*

Review both published in the first days of January. There was an immediate attack on Mivart in *The Tablet* which led him to write to Cardinal Vaughan for an immediate apology. But what had he written to create this storm? He had gone to extremes and written material which was totally modernist or post modernist.

Now for instance infallibility is attacked. He said that the necessary evolution of dogma was impossible unless the errors of past councils could be revoked. In future the Church will encompass all scientific truth and all religious truths held by all the world religions including the old pagan models. As things stood the authority of Rome was stultifying the Church and blocking the need for a dynamic faith, constantly open to change.

Change for Mivart was life itself. In the "Continuity" article he wrote:

> "Catholics to be logical must say to any Roman congregation which should attempt to lay down the law about any branch of science 'you have blundered once (a reference to Galileo) and we can never trust you again in any scientific matter whether it be astronomy,biology, political economy, history, biblical criticism or ecclesiology. You may be right in your dicta but also you may be wrong".

Clearly Mivart would have been much happier living at the close of the 20th century when opponents of the Church's teaching now say almost exactly the same things..only they call it "loyal dissent".

Hensley Henson, later Bishop of Durham, wrote an article entitled "The Mivart Episode" and gives a summary of Mivart's own articles:[10]

> "Dr Mivart assures us that the Roman Church is riddled with unbelief. Even the most rigid of theologians have abandoned the formal creed of the Church with respect to one or other of its articles. ...There is probably no well informed Catholic now in the world who accepts St. Matthew as an interpreter of Prophecy. Many modern Catholics as orthodox as learned

have repudiated the doctrine of atonement and regard Christ's life and death as merely a great object lesson...Another learned theologian assured him that if he could prove that Christ's body had rotted in the grave, the truth of the resurrection would not in the least be affected, and that the doctrine of the Virgin birth is but lightly held."

Such beliefs are quite in line with the view that Mivart had gone indeed beyond Modernism into the post modernist world. Such can also be shown by the strange fact that Cardinal Vaughan urged Mivart to consult with Fr. George Tyrrell SJ. leading modernist in this country and already highly suspect in theology. Tyrrell relates that he could do nothing for Mivart. That is to say that Mivart's theological position was far ahead of Tyrrell's.

Before looking at the exchange of letters between Mivart and Vaughan which followed the publication of the articles one has to ask the question, why did Mivart suddenly adopt such an advanced position.? Gruber suggests that it was inherent in his belief in the supremacy of the individual reason. He could only be intellectually free if he freed himself from external constraints. There is of course some truth in that particularly if we consider the strong influence of Harnack in the next letter quoted below. The alternative is to say that his strong language and apparent loss of faith were due to his illness, a form of diabetes, which he realised was killing him and was causing him increasing bouts of illness including blinding headaches. The question arose at his death about whether he was in his right mind. In some ways the case is quite similar to that of Fr. George Tyrrell, who was suffering from Bright's disease (a liver complaint) and also suffered blinding headaches at the end. Like Mivart his final letters are quite uncharacteristically violent.

Adolf von Harnack (1851-1930) was professor of Church History at Berlin University. He aimed to replace theological dogmatism by historical understanding and attempted to show that the Gospel of Jesus had nothing in common with the authoritarian statutes which became embodied in the doctrines of the Church. If the Church was to survive it had to free itself from these dogmas and seek to return to the basic simplicity of the early Church.

With that in mind it is interesting to see what Mivart wrote to Edmund Bishop at the start of this final crisis (7th Jan. 1900)

> "As long ago as 1892 at Gasquet's recommendation, the reading of Boissieres "Religion Romaine"..produced a great effect on me seeming to make it clear that the triumph of Christianity was an inevitable natural process. Subsequently Weizacker's "Apostolic Years" and Harnack's "History of Dogma" carried my process of mental evolution much further. After reading Harnack I have been studying him in detail and was at it just before I was taken ill on December 2nd. To me now the whole of christianity and processes of the Church are natural processess but as being always a sincere theist, everything and every process is also supernatural. The result as a whole does not seem to matter much. I remain as I consider a Catholic,but a Catholic who wants to make Catholicity as Catholic as possible and to include and accept all truth undyingly.....The Divinity of Christ, the Trinity, the adorability of the Eucharist, the veneration of Christ's mother, and the saints etc all remain acceptable. I can go to Mass as devoutly and worship as truly as ever. If I could make you fully apprehend my position you would think I am in a realm of curious phantasy....as I said I love my friends and grieve to pain them but as to those who love me not, I care nothing, and fear them not one scrap but defy them to do anything against me."

Meanwhile Cardinal Vaughan had already written to Bishop on the 2nd Jan 1900 to thank him for trying to bring Mivart back to a true faith, but admitting that he had been told by a priest who knew him that Mivart had ceased to believe in Christianity for over two years.

The idea of excommunication was already in his head when he wrote in this letter. "It is better for the body that poisonous and deadly humours should be got out lest the whole become infected." [11]

The Cardinal received Mivart's letter of complaint on January 9th and wrote back acknowledging the receipt and adding:

"You have publicly impugned the most sacred and fundamental doctrines of the faith, while still professing yourself to be a Catholic. It becomes, therefore my primary duty as guardian of the Faith to ascertain whether I am still to treat you as a member of the Church and subject to my jurisdiction or to conisder you outside the unity of the Faith. As a test of orthodoxy regardiing certain doctrines dealt with by you in your articles in the" 19th century", I herewith send you a profession of Catholic Faith. I invite you to read and return it to me subscribed by your signature. Nothing less than this will be satisfactory..."

The document enclosed was a standard profession with a section added dealing with Mivart personally. He was asked to sign up to

"I reject as false and heretical the assertion that it is possible at some time according to the progress of science to give to the doctrines propounded by the Church, a sense different from that which the Church has understood them and understands them now and consequently that the sense and meaning of her doctrines can never be in the course of time..reversed. I condemn and revoke all the other words and statements which in articles contributed by me to the *Fornightly Review* and the *Ninetheeth Century*, or in any other of my writings are found to be in a matter of faith and morals contrary to the teaching of the Holy Catholic Faith, according to the determination of the apostolic See; and in such matters I submit myself to the judgement of the said See, receiving all that it receives and condemning all that it condemns."

There followed an exchange of three letters. Mivart refused initially to sign anything unless he received an apology in the *Tablet*, plus a letter from His Eminence and the writer of the offending article asking for pardon.

The Archbishop's final letter to Mivart on January 16th read,

"I regret that I must call upon you a third and last

time to forward to me, with your signature attached thereto, the form of profession of Faith which as your Bishop, I felt bound to send to you.in consequence of your articles..And at the same time I require you to epxress your reprobation of those articles and your sincere sorrow for having published thm. I cannot allow you to evade this duty on the ground of anything that may have been written in the *Tablet*. If you have a grievance against the *Tablet*, You must go to the Editor. I am responsible neither for its language nor its arguments. My dealing with you is exclusively as your Ordinary and Guardian of the Faith of my flock. Failing dutiful submission on your part, the law of the Church will take its course."

Mivart was ill again just then and Gasquet relates in his diary[12] for the 16th Jan. "I got Mivart to see a priest and receive Extreme Unction. It would add to the terrors of Catholic Life if there was to be excommunication by leading article."

So Mivart's reply is dated 23rd Jan. "I categorically refuse to sign the profession of faith..happily I can now speak with entire frankness as to all my convictions. 'Liberavi meam Animam'. I can sign my Nunc Dimittis and calmly await the future".

The Cardinal then addressed the following to his clergy:

"Mivart has declared or seemed to declare that it is possible for Catholics to hold certain heresies regarding the Virginal Birth, the perpetual Virginity, the Gospel account of the Resurrection, the immunity of the sacred Body from corruption, the reality of the trnsmission of original sin, the redemption as a real satisfaction for the sins of men, the everlasting punishment of the wicked, the inspiration and integrity of sacred scripture...I hereby inhibit him from approaching the sacraments and forbid my priests to adminster them to him until he shall have proved his orthodoxy.."

Mivart's reply of the 23rd January is the last letter he wrote to Vaughan. It is 16 pages long and is another apologia for his actions.Here are the key sections.

"I greatly desire to state plainly and to make your Eminence clearly understand what my religion is and what is has for some years been. As you will know, I was once an ardent advocate for Catholicism.

The best years of my life have been spent in its defence while all I said in its favour was most thoroughly meant. Though like many others who thought much on such subjects, I have occassionally passed through periods of doubt and yet for years I was on the whole happy and full of confidence in the position I had taken and which was clearly expressed in my article "The Catholic Church and Biblical Criticism" published in *Nineteenth Century* in July 1887. There I wrote much on the teaching of Cardinal Newman which gave me to understand that Catholics were free only to hold as inspired in some undefined sense of the word, certain portions or parts of the books set before them as 'canonical'. I found great latitude of scriptural interpretation to be not uncommon amongst Catholics both clerical and lay, and my efforts seemed to meet with approbation notably from Pius IX and afterwards to a less degree from Leo XIII.

All of a sudden like a bolt from the blue appeared in 1893 that terrible Encyclical about Scripture known as 'Providentissimus Deus' containing the following unequivocal words 'It is absolutely wrong and forbidden either to narrow inspiration to certain parts only of Holy Scripture or to advocate that the sacred writer has erred.'....It then seemed plain to me that my position was no longer tenable but I had recourse to the most learned theologian I knew and my intimate friend, (presumably Bishop). His representations, distinctions, and exhortations, his great influence upon me more or less satisfied me for a time. But ultimately I came to the conclusion that Catholic Doctrine and Science were totally at variance. This is now more clear than ever since my ordinary does not say whether my judgement about what the attribution of every document in God's authorship involves, is or is not right. To me it is plain that God's veracity and his incapability of deceit are primary truths without which revelation is impossible. This teaching then of Leo XIII addressed dogmatically to the whole Church comes to this 'Every statement made by a canonical writer must be true in the sense in which he put it forward whether as an historical fact or a moral instruction.'

Thus it is now evident that a vast and impassable abyss yawns between Catholic dogma and science and no man with ordinary knowledge can henceforth join the communion of the Catholic Church if he correctly understands what its principles and teaching really are unless they are radically changed. For who could hope to believe the narrative about the tower of Babel, or that all species of animals came up to Adam to be named? Moreover amongst the writings esteemed canonical by the Catholic Church are the book of Tobit and the 2nd book of Maccabees, and also the story which states how when Daniel was thrown a second time into the lions Den, an Angel seized Habacuc in Judea by the hair of his head and carried him with his bowl of pottage to give it to Daniel for his dinner!..To ask a reasonable man to believe such puerile tales would be an insult to him. Still when in two or three years I had become fully convinced that Orthodox Catholicism was untenable, I was extremely disinclined to secede. I was most reluctant to give pain to many dear Catholic friends, some of whom had been very kind to me. My family also is strongly Catholic and my secession might inflict not only great pain but possible social disadvantage on those nearest and dearest to me. Why then I asked myself, should I not continue to conform as advocated in my *Fortnightly Review* article ? Why should I stultify my past career when approaching its end and give myself labour and sorrow? It was a great temptation. Probably I should have remained silent had I not by my writings influenced many persons in favour of what I now felt to be erroneous and therefore inevitably more or less hurtful. To such persons I was a debtor. I also hated to disguise even by reticence what I held to be the truth.

These considerations were brought to a climax last year by a grave and prolongued illness. I was told I would probably die. Could I go out of the world while still remaining silent? It was plain to me I ought not and as soon as I could, (in August) I wrote my recently published articles. Therein I felt it would be useless to confine myself to the question which was for me at the root of the matter, ie Holy Scripture. Therefore...I made my articles as startling as I could in other respects, so as to compel attention to them to elicit if possible an unequivocal pronouncement.

In this I have thank God succeeded and the clause about Scripture I am required to sign is for me decisive. I categorically refuse to sign the profession of faith. Nevertheless I am as I said attached to Catholicity as I understand it and in that I adhere. If then my recent articles had been tolerated, especially my representation as to the probability of more future changes through doctrinal evolution, I would have remained quiet in the hope that little by little I might successfully oppose points I had before mistakenly advocated."

With that all communication dried up between himself and sadly too with Edmund Bishop. His death occurred suddenly at his home on April 1st just as he was about to go out and address a meeting. During the time between January 16th and his death he was totally out of contact with the Church and so died without the sacraments. He was then buried in unconsecrated ground at Kensal Green cemetery. That however is not quite the end of the story.

EPILOGUE

The Archives of the Archdiocese of Westminster contain the file which gives all the letters exchanged between Mivart and Vaughan at the end of Mivart's life and the later correspondence concerning his reburial. Yet there still remains an element of mystery over the circumstances of his original burial. There is a document in the file under the heading "Case of Dr. Mivart" and clearly written by a contemporary which gives an outline of the case. In Point 2 of 8 points listed by number we read

"Cardinal Vaughan was in duty bound to take cognisance of the articles in question and to take action of a decisive kind in the matter. This was his obvious duty as Ordinary of the Diocese in which the Articles were published and as judge in the first instance of matters of faith. Besides we have reason to know that the Cardinal was impelled by higher authority to move in the affair on account of the great scandal caused by the articles."

Then in Point 5 we find:

"Shortly after, Dr Mivart died rather suddenly, and there arose the question of his receiving or being refused burial in consecrated ground. It was contended that Dr. Mivart had not been quite responsible for many things he had said and written during a considerable time before his death and it was asserted that undeniable proof of this contention was in existence. The Cardinal very properly insisted on being furnished with the documents by which this could be proved but Dr. Mivart's friends persisted in witholding them from His Eminence" and in Point 7 "Subsequently Arbishop Bourne (who succeeded Vaughan at Westminster) was supplied with the proofs of Dr. Mivart's irresponsibility and granted Christian or Catholic burial. "

and in point 8:

"Cardinal Vaughan would have done the same had he been put in possession of the documents communicated to Archbishop Bourne some years afterwards."

This account is to put it mildly somewhat deficient in the truth. Item 22 in the file is a letter of Dr. Broadbent a distinguished physician. The letter is dated on the 6th April, a few days after the death of Mivart but after he had already sent the necessary information to Vaughan. It reads:

"The facts are these. I was on terms of friendship with the late Dr. Mivart for many years and his habitual advisor. He has suffered from diabetes for some time and during the last two or three years there has been a painful change in his character.His conduct has been such in several respects that I have many times told Mrs Mivart and their son that I considered him to be practically insane. I had even gone so far to hope that the heart disease which had been coming on for some years, might prove fatal before any public scandal occurred. On this account I did not read any of his recent articles. Young Dr. Mivart knowing my opinion, came to me when the question as to his father's burial arose, and I wrote the letter which Your Eminence has returned hoping that thereby poor Mrs Mivart might be spared further suffering. I did not mark it private as I had confidence in Your Eminence's discretion. I now write more fully for Your Eminence's personal information but as the frank letter appears to have failed in the object for which it was wirtten I think I had better return it. I beg to remain

Your Eminence's Faithful Servant. W.F. Broadbent.

There is no trace of the first letter referred to here in the archive file, but there is a letter (No 23 in file) from a priest of the diocese but apparently unsigned to "My Dear John" presumably J.G. Snead-Cox, the biographer of Vaughan for use in his biography.

> "It is difficult to find time to write, whilst this mission is going on so I must answer your question in just a word now, and promise to call on you when I return home - for I expect you want the information for your book. Cardinal Vaughan sent for me to have my opinion as to whether in view of the certificates the burial in Catholic ground might be permitted, but I did not get the message till too late, and had no part in the decision come to. But I understood that it was as you suspect. The Cardinal asked if he might publish the certificates and, the Mivart's not consenting to this, he felt he could not give a permission which he could not publicly justify. Had the news of the request made and of the certificates got out is another question. Some one leaked, and Dr. F. Mivart was naturally indignant. If you are asking with a view to the life, I should think the less said about this point the better. But please do not bring my name in."

Now the Westminster file does not contain any letter from Dr.F. Mivart to Vaughan at that time, but assuming such a letter was written or a meeting took place one can say with some certainty that the certificate from Dr. Broadbent was presented to Vaughan who asked an expert to judge on its merit but then also asked Dr.F.Mivart for permission to publish the certificates to the press in order that no scandal be given by holding a Catholic burial service. Some inkling of what was happening got out and the Mivart's refused to allow the publication of the document of Dr. Broadbent. So no Catholic funeral was allowed. The absence of certain key letters in the correspondence regrettably suggests some kind of cover up.

Matters were however put right when Archbishop Bourne succeeded to the See of Westminster.

On the 17th January 1904 Everard Green, Rouge Dragon Pursuivant, wrote from the Herald's College.

> "..When may I come and see Your Grace about my dear old friend the late St.G.Mivart F.R.S. and his Christian burial ? The certificate you asked for I have obtained from Professor Pepper MS London F.R.C.S. Surgeon and lecturer in Surgery at St Mary's Hospital, Paddington who was an intimate friend of Professor Mivart's for some twenty years. If your Grace would like the opinion of a cleric, Abbot Gasquet allows me to say that he will be very pleased to come and see you and to show you the last letters Mivart wrote to him..."

The letter then adds an enclosure from Dr. Pepper. The key passage from his testimony reads:

> "During the last four or five years of his life I noticed he was the subject of senile decay which manifested itself in thought and action quite at variance with his former self. In my opinion he ought not to be considered as altogether accountable for what he wrote during these years."

Bourne himself wrote on the blank side of this letter:

> "Everard Green called to see on Sunday Jan 3rd 1904 and on the strength of this certificate I gave permission for the body of the late Dr. Mivart to be transferred to consecrated ground. I heard from Cardinal Vaughan's lips that he was prepared to give this permission on the production of such a certificate."

One can only conclude that Dr. Broadbent's original

testimony had not come down to Cardinal Bourne.

On the 18th January 1904 Everard Green wrote again.

> "Duty devotion and desire bid me write and tell Your Grace that the Requiem Mass and internment afterwards of my dear old friend Mr St. G. Mivart F.R.S. took place this morning at half past ten. The only son, Mrs Frederick Mivart and myself were the only mourners, and we had the chapel and cemetery to ourselves as no one was about. The service was very quiet and nicely performed and the Mass said (for a wonder) clara voce so we actually HEARD Mass which is somewhat rare today."

A further letter in the file tells us that Mivart's widow was too ill to attend, but she thanks Archbishop Bourne profusely for his kindness. The Archbishop then put out a statement in the press.

> "The Archbishop of Westminster having received convincing medical assurance that the opinions expressed by the late Professor St.George Mivart towards the close of his life in no way represented his real and normal attitude of mind but resulted from failure of mental powers consequent upon his illness, has allowed his remains to be removed to the family grave in the Catholic Cemetery at Kensal Green. This translation took place more than a fortnight ago. Low Mass of Requiem was celebrated before the last funeral rites were performed. No other ceremony is contemplated."

NOTES AND SOURCES.

The only biography of Mivart so far written is entitled *A Conscience in Conflict* by Jacob W.Gruber, Columba University Press, New York, 1960. The only real biographical detail we have of his early life comes from an article in the Dublin Review, *Early Memories of St.George Mivart*. 1924, This is an edited version of autobiographical notes handed on by Mivart to his son Frederick. Gruber does not accept the view that illness clouded Mivart's judgement. Although he mentions briefly the fact of reburial, he gives no details of the circumstances. It is only fair to Mivart's memory that the full facts be presented and the reader can judge whether he was deranged or not. Mivart's considerable literary output is listed in the Dictionary of National Biography entry. This essay only considers his theological musings as they affected his faith. A considerable quantity of his letters survive, notably to Edmund Bishop and Alice Meynell.

1) The biographical details for this chapter are taken from Gruber Chapter 1. The detail of his friendship with Fr.Spencer is not given by Gruber but comes from the Dublin Review article.
2) Archives of the Diocese of Southwark. Bishop Danell Papers.
3) *Contemporary Evolution* London 1876 See Gruber pp148-155
4) Ward's original article is in *Dublin Review* LXXIX 1876 page 3 Professor Mivart on the Rights of Conscience while the reply of Dr Mivart is entitled *Liberty of Conscience* in D.R. same volume page 563ff.
5) Newman to Mivart May 28th 1876 Quoted by Gruber p 1546) Newman to Mivart March 6th 1884 Quoted by Gruber p 158
7) Newman to Mivart May 9th 1884 Quoted by Gruber p 163
8) R.F.Clarke's reply was first published as an article in *Nineteenth Century* 1893 No 33 page 83ff.
9) The letters between Edmund Bishop and Mivart are in the Archives...at Downside but were published by Nigel Abercrombie in an article entitled *Edmund Bishop and St.George Mivart* in the MONTH 1952 Page 176ff.
10) Herbert Hensley Henson, *The Mivart Episode* This appeared in the *Nineteeth Century Magazine*. I do not have the date. The article was discovered in a set of pamphlets on Mivart at Downside.
11) Much of the correspondence between Mivart and Vaughan was later published in New York in a volume

entitled *Under the Ban* .

I also used the original documents in the Westminster Diocesan Archives for my compilation here as with the documents relating to his reburial.

12) Shane Leslie. *Cardinal Gasquet- A Memoir*, London 1952 page 185

INDEX

SELECTED BIBLIOGRAPHY

Besides the works listed in the Text and Notes, the following books may be considered as good background material.

For the Period 1830 to 1850 in General
" Sequel to Catholic Emancipation" by Bernard Ward. 2vols London, 1915

For the Oxford Movement in Particular.
"The Mind of the Oxford Movement" by Owen Chadwick London 1963
"The Oxford Movement in Context" by Peter Benedict Nockles, Cambridge, 1994

For the Liberal Catholic Movement."The Liberal Catholic Movement in England, the Rambler and its Contributors" Joseph Altholz London 1962

For Cardinal Wiseman's Life.
"Nicholas Wiseman" by Richard Schieffen, Sheperdstown USA. 1984

For Cardinal Manning.
"Cardinal Manning" by Robert Gray, London 1985
"Cardinal Manning" by Vincent Alan McClelland, London 1962.

For Cardinal Newman.
"Newman and His Age" by Sheridan Gilley, London 1990
"John Henry Newman - A Biography" by Fr.Ian Ker Oxford.1988

For comparison of Newman and Manning.
"The Convert Cardinals" by David Newsome, London 1993.

(This is only a very small selection of the books available on the topics covered. A far wider bibliography can be had from the lists given in most of the books mentioned above).